Battle in the Wilderness
Grant Meets Lee

D1052519

CIVIL WAR CAMPAIGNS AND COMMANDERS SERIES

AVAILABLE SPRING 1995

Texans in the Confederate Cavalry by Anne J. Bailey
Death in September: The Antietam Campaign
  by Perry D. Jamieson
Sam Bell Maxey and the Confederate Indians by John C. Waugh

FORTHCOMING TITLES, FALL 1995

General James Longstreet in the West: A Monumental Failure
  by Judith Lee Hallock
Battle of the Crater by Jeff Kinard
The Saltville Massacre by Tom Mays

Battle in the Wilderness
Grant Meets Lee

Grady McWhiney

RYAN PLACE PUBLISHERS
FORT WORTH

Cataloging-in-Publication Data

McWhiney, Grady.
    Battle in the Wilderness: Grant meets Lee / by Grady McWhiney.
    p. cm.
    Includes bibliographical references and index.
    ISBN: 1-886661-00-6

    1. Wilderness, Battle of the, VA., 1864.   I. Title

    E476.52.M39 1995   973.7'36
                                 QBI94-21300

Copyright © 1995, Ryan Place Publishers, Inc.

All Rights Reserved

2730 Fifth Avenue
Fort Worth, Texas 76110

No part of this book may be reproduced in any form or by any means
without permission in writing from Ryan Place Publishers, Inc.

Printed in the United States of America

ISBN 1-886661-00-6
10 9 8 7 6 5 4 3 2 1

Book Designed by Rosenbohm Design Group

We gratefully acknowledge the assistance of the Library of Congress, from whose
collection all except one of the photographs in this book have been reproduced.
For the photograph of Alfred Moore Scales we acknowledge the North Carolina State
Department of Cultural Resources.

All inquiries regarding volume purchases of this book should be
addressed to Ryan Place Publishers, Inc., 4709 Colleyville Boulevard,
Suite 580, Colleyville, TX 76034-3985. Telephone inquiries may be made
by calling 817-421-9382.

A NOTE ON THE SERIES

Few segments of America's past excite more interest than Civil War battles and leaders. This ongoing series of brief, lively, and authoritative books–*Civil War Campaigns and Commanders*–salutes this passion with inexpensive and accurate accounts that are readable in a sitting. Each volume, separate and complete in itself, nevertheless conveys the agony, glory, death, and wreckage that defined America's greatest tragedy.

In this series, designed for Civil War enthusiasts as well as the newly recruited, emphasis is on telling good stories. Photographs and biographical sketches enhance the narrative of each book, and maps depict events as they happened. Sound history is meshed with the dramatic in a format that is just lengthy enough to inform and yet satisfy.

Grady McWhiney
General Editor

CONTENTS

CAMPAIGNS AND COMMANDERS SERIES

Map Key

Geography

Trees

Marsh

Fields

Strategic Elevations

Rivers

Tactical Elevations

Fords

Orchards

Political Boundaries

Human Construction

Bridges

Railroads

Tactical Towns

Strategic Towns

Buildings

Church

Roads

Military

Union Infantry

Confederate Infantry

Cavalry

Artillery

Headquarters

Encampments

Fortifications

Permanant Works

Hasty Works

Obstructions

Engagements

Warships

Gunboats

Casemate Ironclad

Monitor

  Tactical Movements

Strategic Movements

Maps by
Donald S. Frazier, PhD.
Abilene, Texas

MAPS

PHOTOGRAPHS

Battle in the Wilderness
Grant Meets Lee

1

ROADS TO THE WILDERNESS

In May 1864 General Ulysses S. Grant moved a huge Federal army into an area of Virginia west of Fredericksburg known as the Wilderness, which he only wanted to use as a passageway. Rather than attack General Robert E. Lee's army, entrenched along the south bank of the Rapidan River, Grant planned to force Lee out of his strong defensive position, compelling him either to fight on terrain selected by the Federals or to fall back toward the Confederate capital in Richmond.

Grant's plan failed. Instead of retreating southward, Lee struck the Federals as they marched through the Wilderness, thus neutralizing much of Grant's advantage in manpower. After two days of hard fighting, more than 18,000 Federals and nearly 11,000 Confederates were dead, wounded, or missing. But the Wilderness was merely the opening action in a deadly

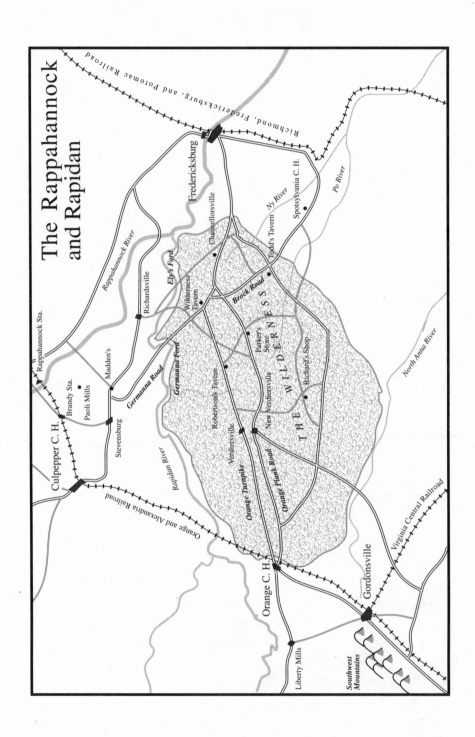

The Rappahannock and Rapidan

General Robert E. Lee Born Virginia 1807; son of Ann Hill (Carter) Lee and Henry "Light-Horse Harry" Lee, who died when Robert was eleven; received early education in Alexandria, Va., schools; graduated second in his class at U.S. Military Academy in 1829, without receiving a demerit in four years; appointed 2d lieutenant of engineers in 1829, 1st lieutenant in 1836, and captain in 1838. Served at Fort Pulaski, Fort Monroe, Fort Hamilton, and superintended engineering project for St. Louis harbor; married Mary Ann Randolph Custis, whose father's estate of "Arlington" on the Virginia shore of the Potomac opposite Washington became Lee's home in 1857 after the death of his father-in-law. In 1846 Lee, then a captain, joined General Winfield Scott's Vera Cruz expedition and invasion of Mexico; Lee's extraordinary industry and capacity won him a brilliant reputation and the lasting confidence and esteem of Scott; wounded in 1847, Lee won three brevet promotions to major, lieutenant colonel, and colonel for gallant and meritorious conduct in the battles of Cerro Gordo, Contreras, Churubusco, and Chapultepec. Served as superintendent of the U.S. Military Academy from 1852 to 1855; promoted to lieutenant colonel 2d Cavalry in 1855; commanded marines sent to Harper's Ferry to capture John Brown after his raid; promoted to colonel 1st Cavalry in 1861. Having refused command of Federal armies, his first Confederate command led to failure at Cheat Mountain in western Virginia; after serving along the South Atlantic coast, he returned to Virginia as military adviser to President Jefferson Davis until June 1862 when he replaced the wounded Joseph

E. Johnston in command of forces that became known as the Army of Northern Virginia. For nearly three years, Lee's aggressive campaigns and effective defenses frustrated Union efforts to capture the Confederate capital; not until February 1865—two months before his surrender—did he become overall commander of Confederate forces. After the war, he accepted the presidency of Washington College (later changed to Washington and Lee University) in Lexington, Va., where he remained until his death in 1870. Theodore Roosevelt proclaimed Lee "without exception the very greatest of all the great captains." Bold, modest, and heroic, Lee once confessed that if war were not so terrible he would become too fond of it. His greatest biographer characterized him as "a simple gentleman."

series of battles for control of Virginia that lasted nearly a year and ended only with Lee's surrender.

Before their encounter in the Wilderness, Lee and Grant had enjoyed remarkable Civil War careers. In June 1862, with a large Union army threatening the Confederate capital, Lee had assumed command of what became known as the Army of Northern Virginia, relieving the wounded Joseph E. Johnston after the Battle of Fair Oaks or Seven Pines. Lee removed the Federal threat in the Seven Days' Battle by driving Union forces across the Peninsula to the James River south of Richmond. He then divided his army, sending General Thomas J. "Stonewall" Jackson to northern Virginia to oppose a new Federal army, and joining him in August with the rest of the army in time to rout the Federals at Second Manassas. Lee followed that success by invading Maryland, but withdrew in September after fighting the bloodiest single day of the war at Antietam or Sharpsburg. Just before 1862 ended, he turned back another Federal invasion of Virginia by defeating a large Union army at Fredericksburg.

The following spring Lee won a brilliant but costly victory over another large Federal army at Chancellorsville. Ignoring military precedent, he divided his army, threatened the Federal left, and boldly sent Jackson's Corps on a flanking march through the same Wilderness where Lee and Grant would meet a year later. Just before dark on May 2, 1863, Jackson surprised and drove back the exposed Federal right flank. When nightfall ended the fighting, Jackson rode to the front trying to determine how close his and Lee's troops were to linking up. As he and his escort returned to camp, Confederate soldiers fired on Jackson and his staff, whom they mistook for Federal cavalry, mortally wounding the general. The battle continued the next day, but on May 4 the Federals ended the contest and withdrew.

Lee's next campaign, another invasion of the North, ended

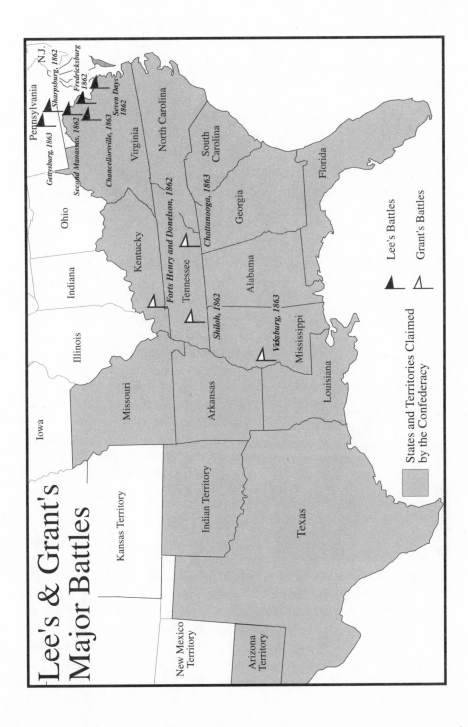

Lee's & Grant's Major Battles

disastrously in July at Gettysburg. After three days of hard fighting and heavy losses, Lee retreated to northern Virginia, where he awaited a new Federal advance.

After Gettysburg neither Lee nor the Confederacy were ever the same. Forced to be less bold after the summer of 1863, Lee relied more on defense. Attrition and his inability to replace his losses had deprived him of sufficient manpower to make sustained assaults. He fought a brilliant defensive campaign during the last months of the Civil War, making the Federals pay in casualties for each of their gains.

When Lee met Grant in the Wilderness, they were headed

General Ulysses S. Grant Born Ohio 1822; graduated U.S. Military Academy 1843, twenty-first in his class; brevetted 2d lieutenant in 4th Infantry 1843; 2d lieutenant 1845; 1st lieutenant 1847; regimental quartermaster 1847 to 1853; brevetted captain 1847 for gallant conduct in Mexican War; assigned in 1852 to duty in  California, where he missed his wife and drank heavily. Resigned from army in 1854 to avoid court martial; failed at a number of undertakings; appointed colonel 21st Illinois Infantry and then brigadier general volunteers in 1861; major general volunteers 1862; gained national attention following victories at Fort Donelson, Shiloh, and Vicksburg; received thanks of Congress and promotion to major general U.S. Army in 1863; after victories around Chattanooga, appointed lieutenant general and commander of all U.S. forces in 1864. Accompanied Meade's Army of the Potomac on a bloody campaign of attrition through the Wilderness, Spotsylvania, Cold Harbor, siege of Petersburg, and the pursuit to Appomattox; commander of the U.S. Army 1864 to 1869; U.S. president 1869 to 1877. Visited Europe, suffered bankruptcy, and wrote his memoirs while dying of cancer; died in 1885 in New York City, where he is buried. "The art of war is simple enough," Grant once explained. "Find out where your enemy is. Get at him as soon as you can. Strike at him as hard as you can, and keep moving on." A staff officer said of Grant: "His face has three expressions: deep thought, extreme determination, and great simplicity and calmness."

in different directions. Lee's great successes had been in the past; the future belonged to Grant. He did not have to outfight Lee in the last year of the war; he simply overwhelmed him with men and guns.

During the war's first three years, Grant's successes in the West had equalled, if not surpassed, Lee's impressive record in the East. In 1862 Grant, with the help of Union gunboats, broke the Confederate western defense line across northern Tennessee by capturing Forts Henry and Donelson. The loss of these and other river forts opened the Cumberland, Tennessee, and Mississippi rivers as invasion routes into the Deep South.

His victory at Shiloh in April 1862 checked a Confederate counteroffensive and inspired other Federal successes in the West. Union forces not only turned back invasions of New Mexico, Missouri, and Kentucky; they invaded Arkansas, Tennessee, Mississippi, and Louisiana; captured Nashville, Memphis, and New Orleans; and pinched the middle of the Confederacy from both ends. Grant's failure to take Vicksburg late in 1862 had been one of the Union's few setbacks in the West; indeed, Federal gains during the year had been impressive. Among their successes: significant progress toward opening the Mississippi River, a stronger naval blockade of southern ports, and the occupation of parts of western Virginia, Kentucky, Missouri, most of Tennessee, portions of Mississippi and Louisiana, and half of Arkansas. In battles won and lost, Union armies had done better in the West and Confederate armies better in the East. On both sides casualties had been staggering. The Confederates had lost more men than they could replace, but remained dangerous.

In the spring of 1863, Grant began another effort to capture Vicksburg. Four previous attempts had failed, but this plan appeared promising. After Union gunboats successfully slipped past the Vicksburg batteries and ferried Federal troops from Louisiana across the Mississippi River south of the town,

Grant moved east, defeated fragmentary Confederate opposition, and captured Jackson, the state capital. Turning his attention back to Vicksburg, he besieged the town when his attack on the strong Confederate defenses failed. On July 4, after a siege of forty-two days, 29,000 Confederate soldiers and thousands of starving civilians surrendered. Grant had won a major victory, which together with the Union's successful siege of Port Hudson, Louisiana, cut the Confederacy in two. The Federals had control of the entire Mississippi River.

The fall of Vicksburg and the defeat of Lee at Gettysburg restored confidence in the North. The Union navy had closed all the important Confederate Atlantic ports except Charleston, South Carolina, and Wilmington, North Carolina, and these were blockaded by Federal warships. A Union amphibious expedition threatened Charleston, and Federal forces captured Chattanooga and pushed into north Georgia.

To meet this threat, President Davis sent General James Longstreet's Corps from Lee's army to reinforce the Confederate army in northern Georgia. On September 19 the Confederates attacked near Chickamauga Creek, and the following day routed the Federals, who retreated to Chattanooga.

Taking positions on the heights south of Chattanooga, the Confederates besieged the city. But their attempt to starve the Federals into surrendering—as the Confederates had been forced to do at Vicksburg—failed when Grant, now Union commander in the West, opened the supply line into Chattanooga. Late in November Grant's men drove the Rebels from Lookout Mountain and Missionary Ridge, the heights commanding Chattanooga. Badly defeated, the Confederates retreated into Georgia.

News of Grant's victory at Chattanooga reached the North on Thanksgiving Day. The year 1863 had begun glumly, but

Northerners now felt hopeful after their tremendous victories at Vicksburg, Gettysburg, and Chattanooga. With the entire Mississippi Valley under Federal control, Union armies had an open gateway into the central Confederacy. Many Northerners now believed that Confederate power had been broken. "The crisis," said President Abraham Lincoln, "which threatens to divide the friends of the Union is past." Events seemed to justify such optimism, yet hard fighting remained.

2

WHAT MANNER OF MEN

In February 1864 Congress revived the military rank of lieutenant general and authorized the president to promote to that rank the major general most distinguished for courage, skill, and ability. Grant's victories at Vicksburg and Chattanooga convinced Lincoln that he had finally found the man who might destroy the Confederacy. He called Grant to the capital and not only gave him command of all Union forces, but appointed him a lieutenant general in the regular army, a rank previously held only by George Washington and Winfield Scott.

Scott, known as "Old Fuss and Feathers," had distinguished himself in both the War of 1812 and the Mexican War. His ideas and campaigns influenced a generation of young Mexican War officers, including Lee and Grant. Now too old and ill for field command, Scott had proposed at the war's outset "the Anaconda plan" of blockading southern ports, gaining control of the Mississippi River, and then "squeezing" the South into submission.

Grant resembled neither Washington nor Scott in manner or physique. Colonel Charles S. Wainwright, chief of artillery for the Union Fifth Corps, complained that at a review "Grant rode along the line in a slouchy unobservant way, with his coat unbuttoned and setting anything but an example of military bearing to the troops." Furthermore, confessed Wainwright, "It is hard for those [of us] who knew him in the [old] army to believe that he is a great man; then he was only distinguished for the mediocrity of his mind, his great good nature and his insatiable love of whiskey." Another observer reported that Grant had "no gait, no station, no manner," only "the look of a man who [took] a little too much to drink"; he seemed "ordinary, scrubby, [and] slightly seedy, as if he was out of office on half pay."

As befitting an "ordinary" man, Grant began making plans without fanfare. He visited various generals in the East and even returned to Tennessee to confer with his closest confidant, General William T. Sherman, the man Grant had selected to replace him as commander of Federal forces in the West. When Grant described the eastern troops as "the finest army he had ever seen, far superior to ours," Sherman begged his friend "to be yourself—simple, honest and unpretending"— and not to let the politicians know what he was about. Sherman told his brother, Senator John Sherman: "[Grant] ought not to trust even Mr. Lincoln, and as to a member of Congress I hope Grant will make it a death penalty for one to go south of the Potomac."

A Union officer recalled that Grant and Sherman were as unlike as day and night: "Grant had no nerves, while Sherman was made up of nerves. Grant never gave himself any concern in regard to an enemy he could not see, while a concealed foe was more dreadful to Sherman than one in full view. Grant's strategy consisted in getting as near an enemy as possible, and then 'moving on his works without delay.' Sherman was more of a strategist, and believed in surprising his enemy by a masterly move. Grant reached Richmond by more fighting than strategy. Sherman reached Atlanta by more strategy than fighting."

Grant outlined his strategy to Sherman. First, he intended to prevent the Confederates from using their interior lines to

General William T. Sherman Born Ohio 1820; graduated from U.S. Military Academy 1840, sixth in his class; 2d lieutenant 3rd Artillery 1840; 1st lieutenant 1841; stationed in California during Mexican War; captain 1850. Resigned from army 1853 to become banker; after business failed, Sherman voluntarily assumed personal financial responsibility for money lost by his friends; practiced law for a

short time in Kansas, losing only case he tried; from 1859 to 1861 superintendent of military college that later became Louisiana State University. Colonel 13th Infantry and then brigadier general volunteers 1861; commanded brigade at First Bull Run; commanded division at Shiloh; major general volunteers 1862 to 1864, serving under Grant in the Vicksburg and Chattanooga campaigns; brigadier general U.S. Army 1863; major general 1864; assumed direction of principal military operations in the West. Directed Meridian and Atlanta campaigns, March to the Sea, and Carolina campaign that ended in surrender of Joseph E. Johnston's army in 1865; received thanks of Congress "for gallant and arduous services" during the Civil War; lieutenant general 1866; general 1869; commander of the army 1869 to 1883; retired 1883; published memoirs 1875; died 1891. Made his famous statement, "war is all hell," in a speech at Columbus, Ohio, in 1880. An officer noted that Sherman's "features express determination, particularly the mouth. He is a very homely man, with a regular nest of wrinkles in his face, which play and twist as he eagerly talks on each subject; but his expression is pleasant and kindly." Some authorities rate him an even better general than Grant.

shift troops and resources to more threatened areas. In the past, Grant noted, "various [Union] armies had acted separately and independently of each other, giving the enemy an opportunity to reinforce [Rebel armies that were] more actively engaged. I determined to stop this [and] to concentrate

General George G. Meade Born Spain of U.S. parents 1815; graduated from U.S. Military Academy 1835, nineteenth in his class; appointed 2d lieutenant 3rd Artillery 1835; resigned in 1836 to become a civil engineer; reentered army in 1842 as 2d lieutenant Topographical Engineers; brevet 1st lieutenant 1846 for gallant conduct during Mexican War; 1st lieutenant 1851; captain 1856. Appointed brigadier general volunteers 1861; advanced from command of a brigade during the Seven Days (wounded in White Oak Swamp) and Second Bull

Run to command of a division at Antietam and Fredericksburg, to command of the Fifth Corps at Chancellorsville; brigadier general U.S. Army 1863. Selected by President Lincoln to replace Joseph Hooker as commander of Army of the Potomac, Meade fought at Gettysburg only two days after assuming army command; major general 1864; received thanks of Congress in 1864 for his contributions to Union victory. From the Wilderness to Appomattox, Meade was in the awkward position of commanding the Army of the Potomac while Grant, the overall commander, traveled with Meade's army. After the war, he commanded first the Division of the Atlantic and then Reconstruction Military District No. 3 (comprising Alabama, Georgia, and Florida); bitterly disappointed at not being appointed lieutenant general when Sherman replaced Grant as army commander, Meade returned to command the Division of the Atlantic; died of pneumonia in 1872, never having fully recovered from his White Oak Swamp wound. A staff officer called Meade an "old gentleman with a hooked nose and cold blue eye," who could be a terror. Grant pronounced him "brave and conscientious, [a man who] commanded the respect of all who knew him."

all force possible against the Confederate armies in the field." Grant proposed that Sherman's army in Georgia move southward toward Atlanta, while Grant and General

General Benjamin Franklin Butler Born New Hampshire 1818; graduated in 1838 from Waterbury (now Colby) College in Maine; taught school and studied law; admitted to the bar 1840 and began successful law practice that continued until his death; married Sarah Hildreth, an actress. Elected as a Democrat in 1853 and 1859 to the Massachusetts legislature; in 1860 favored nomination of Jefferson Davis for president, but voted for John C. Breckinridge. Elected brigadier general of Massachusetts militia in 1861 and led 8th Massachusetts Volunteers to relief of Washington; named major general of volunteers in 1861; while at Fort Monroe, he dubbed slaves fleeing Confederate owners to Union lines "contraband," a term that clung to them throughout the war; undertook military expedition at Big Bethel that

ended disastrously, but captured Fort Hatteras and Fort Clark, North Carolina; in 1862 commanded land forces occupying New Orleans, where as military governor he aroused much criticism for his savage acts of repression, including an order that women insulting Union soldiers be treated as prostitutes; for alleged financial irregularities and supposedly stealing a citizen's silverware, Butler received the nickname "Silverspoons." In 1863 he was given command of the Army of the James and of eastern Virginia and North Carolina; in 1864, as prisoner exchange commissioner, Butler somehow got the military status of U.S. black troops recognized, but also got his army bottled up at Bermuda Hundred by inferior numbers of Confederates; sent to New York City in November 1864 to prevent possible riots during the election, he managed to preserve order. Lost his army command by failing to cooperate effectively with the Army of the Potomac and by bungling an attempt to capture Fort Fisher. A prominent Radical Republican in Congress from 1866 until 1875, he managed the impeachment of Andrew Johnson; reelected as a Greenbacker to Congress in 1878, Butler became Democratic governor of Massachusetts in 1882; he died at Washington in 1893.

George G. Meade's army in northern Virginia and General
Benjamin F. Butler's army in eastern Virginia advanced toward
Richmond.

Their long association had given Grant great confidence in
Sherman, and Grant also believed that he could rely on Meade,
and even Butler. Lincoln had misgivings about Meade, who had
failed either to follow up his great victory at Gettysburg or to
initiate a successful campaign against Lee's undermanned
army. From the outset of their association, Grant and Meade
got along well. "I had a great fondness for him," Grant later

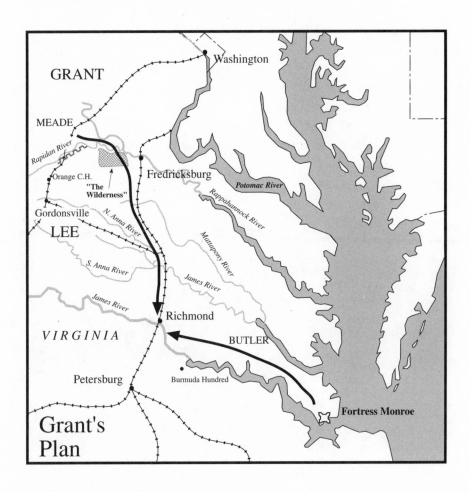

confessed, and Meade wrote his wife: "I was much pleased with Grant." As for Butler, one of Grant's staff officers concluded: "Butler is sharp, shrewd, able [and] over-bearing. A bad man to have against you." Yet Grant believed that he could work with both Meade and Butler. Grant's chief of staff informed his wife: "In Sherman, Meade and Butler, General Grant has three generals, all in important commands, whom he can trust." Rather than remain behind a desk in Washington, Grant decided to establish his headquarters in the field. Meade would retain command of the Army of the Potomac, but Grant would travel with the army and direct its operations. That suited Meade, who found that Grant "agrees so with me in his views, I cannot but be rejoiced at his arrival, because I [now] believe success to be [forthcoming]." His relationship with Meade left Grant free to plan and conduct his own campaigns and to match his military skills against those of the wily Robert E. Lee.

During the upcoming Virginia Campaign, Grant intended to

Confederate Prisoners of War

move southward through the Wilderness as Butler advanced up the James River from Fort Monroe toward Richmond. Grant believed that the capture of Richmond would do more "to break the power of the rebellion" than anything else, "unless it were the capture of Lee's army." If, on the way to Richmond, the Army of the Potomac could destroy Lee's army in the field, so much the better; if not, Grant hoped that Meade and Butler could unite against Lee near the James River. "Lee's army and Richmond being the objects toward which our attention must be directed," observed Grant, "it is desirable to unite all the force against them."

The disaster at Gettysburg and the winter of 1863–64 had taken their toll on Lee's tired army. Nobody realized the seriousness of this situation better than Lee, who no longer enjoyed good health. The prolonged strain of command combined with his multiple responsibilities had weakened the fifty-seven-year-old Lee, just as the rigors and exposures of camp life and the insufficient diet he shared with his men had

sapped his strength. During the winter he had been ill, suffering from violent intestinal disturbances and a heart condition that would kill him in six years. Attacks of sciatica and serious rheumatic back pains also compelled him to take more rest.

Lee revealed the poor state of his health in a letter to President Davis asking to be relieved from command of the Army of Northern Virginia:

> I do this with the most earnestness because no one is more aware than myself of my inability for the duties of my position. I cannot even accomplish what I myself desire. How can I fulfill the expectations of others? In addition I sensibly feel the growing failure of my bodily strength. I have not yet recovered from the attack I experienced the past spring. I am becoming more and more incapable of exertion, and am thus prevented from making the personal examinations and giving the personal supervision to the operations in the field which I feel to be necessary. I am so dull that in making use of the eyes of others I am frequently misled. Everything, therefore, points to the advantages to be derived from a new commander, and I the more anxiously urge the matter upon Your Excellency from my belief that a younger and abler man than myself can readily be attained.

Davis refused to replace Lee, but the general's health continued to decline. During the upcoming campaign against Grant in May and June 1864 Lee would be debilitated for ten days by sickness. His beard and hair whitened, his face showed age, and he no longer moved with the step of youth. But his spirits were high and he seemed ready—indeed, eager—to take on Grant.

General James Longstreet Born South Carolina 1821; graduated U.S. Military Academy fifty-fourth in his class in 1842; appointed a brevet 2d lieutenant in the 4th Infantry in 1842; promoted to 2d lieutenant in the 8th Infantry in 1845 and to 1st lieutenant in 1847; won brevet promotions to captain and major for gallant conduct in the battles of Contreras, Churubusco, and Molino del Rey during the Mexican War; served as regimental adjutant from 1847 to 1849; promoted to captain in 1852 and to major (paymaster department) in 1858. Appointed Confederate brigadier general, served at First Manassas, and promoted to major general in 1861; distinguished service during Peninsular Campaign, Second Manassas, Sharpsburg, and Fredericksburg in 1862; promoted to lieutenant general in 1862, "Old Pete" became General Lee's senior corps commander; on detached service south of the James River in May 1863, thus missing the action at Chancellorsville; commanded right wing of Lee's army at Gettysburg in July 1863; took his corps by rail to Chickamauga, Ga., in September 1863 to help defeat General William S. Rosecrans, but failed in his attempt to capture Knoxville, Tenn. Returned to Virginia in 1864 in time to participate in the Battle of the Wilderness, where he sustained a critical wound that incapacitated him until late fall; led his corps during closing months of the war in defense of Richmond; surrendered with Lee to Grant at Appomattox Court House; after the war, he settled in New Orleans, became a Republican, and led black troops against Confederate veterans during Reconstruction; enjoyed political patronage from Republicans; wrote his war memoirs, *From Manassas to Appomattox*; died at Gainesville, Ga., in 1904. Lee called Longstreet "my old War Horse." An able battlefield tactician, he was at times stubborn, quarrelsome, and overconfident in his ability as an independent commander.

As for the men whom Lee would lead into battle, photographs of captured Confederates reveal as much as any letter or diary about the courage of the ragged soldiers who faced Grant in 1864. These fighters—though deprived of their weapons and anything but "uniform" in their dress—sit with the dignity of accomplishment. To them "Marse Robert" was still the unconquerable commander, the brilliant leader under whom they had so willingly served.

But Lee worried about the declining health of his men. "A regular supply of provisions to the troops in this army is a matter of great importance," he informed the Confederate secretary of war. "Short rations are having a bad effect upon the men, both morally and physically. Desertions to the enemy are becoming more frequent, and the men cannot continue healthy and vigorous if confined to this spare diet for any length of time. Unless there is a change, I fear the army cannot be kept effective, and probably cannot be kept together."

The shortage of food was only one of Lee's many problems. The Army of Northern Virginia's First Corps, commanded by General James Longstreet, had recently returned from winter campaigning in Tennessee. During Longstreet's absence, Lee's other two corps had held a defense line along Mine Run and the Rapidan River that proved too formidable for Meade's army during the Mine Run Campaign late in 1863. Unable to find a weak point in Lee's line, Meade withdrew without attacking and went into winter quarters.

Lee expected Grant to be a new test. "The importance of [the upcoming campaign] to the administration of Mr. Lincoln and to General Grant," Lee wrote President Davis, "leaves no doubt that every effort and every sacrifice will be made to secure its success."

3

CROSSING THE RAPIDAN

Perhaps remembering the failure of his assaults on the Confederate lines at Vicksburg, Grant decided not to attack Lee's entrenched army. Instead, he proposed to cross the Rapidan east of Lee's works and to move around the Confederate right. If all went as Grant planned, Lee would be forced to abandon his defenses and rush southward to prevent the Army of the Potomac from getting between him and Richmond. But in order to turn Lee's right flank, the Federals would have to march through the Wilderness, a dense forest west of Fredericksburg that extended nearly fifteen miles along the south bank of the Rapidan and for ten miles farther south.

Both armies were familiar with this area, having fought in the thick undergrowth during the Battle of Chancellorsville. A Federal officer described the wooded terrain as "hard for even

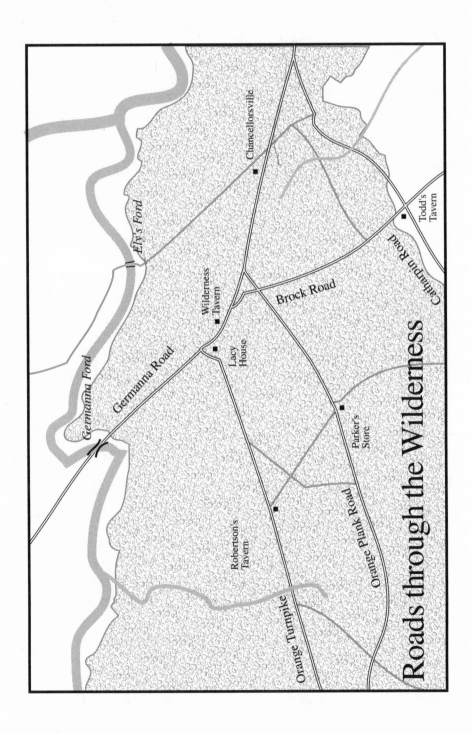

Roads through the Wilderness

a single man to force his way through." There were, he noted, "only two or three roads that can be counted on." The others— "narrow, winding and little known"—could slow a column of wagons and artillery to a crawl even in good weather.

Four roads offered the best access to the Wilderness: the Germanna Plank Road crossed the Rapidan River and the northern part of the Wilderness and linked up with the Brock Road, which continued southward past Todd's Tavern and on to the New Spotsylvania Court House. Running east and west and crossing the Germanna and Brock roads were the Orange Turnpike and the Orange Plank Road. From Orange Court House, where Lee had his headquarters, the Turnpike went to Fredericksburg by way of Chancellorsville; so did the Plank Road, which ran a few miles south and roughly parallel to the Turnpike from Lee's headquarters eastward until it intersected the Turnpike just west of Chancellorsville. If the Army of the Potomac intended to go anywhere in the Wilderness it would have to move north and south on the Germanna and Brock roads and east and west on either the Turnpike or the Plank Road.

The Federals considered the Wilderness something to be crossed as quickly as possible, but Lee regarded it as an ally that would negate some of Grant's numerical advantage in manpower and artillery. The moment Lee learned that Grant's army was moving into the Wilderness, he decided to stop it there.

Grant realized that he might be ambushed while passing through the Wilderness. Fearing the terrain would immobilize his artillery and cavalry and hamper the effective use of his infantry, he hoped a quick march would get the army unscathed through the thick forest. By the time Lee discovered the Federal movement and mounted an attack, Grant expected to be safely out of the Wilderness. As was the case with so many other Federal commanders, he seriously underestimated the ability of his opponent.

Just before the Federals entered the Wilderness, a Maine volunteer confided to his diary: "All of this high planning involves the absurd proposition that Lee will be found napping. But they reckon ill who underestimate Lee; he is said to sleep with one eye open. Though Lee's ranks are decimated and our own have been largely augmented, and we hope for a short and decisive campaign, yet none has the courage to prophesy anything but defeat."

On May 4 the Army of the Potomac moved into the Wilderness in two separate columns. General Gouverneur K. Warren's Fifth Corps and General John Sedgwick's Sixth Corps crossed the Rapidan at Germanna Ford and proceeded southeast along the Germanna Road. Farther east General

Federals Crossing the Rapidan River on Pontoons at Germanna Ford into the Wilderness

General Gouverneur K. Warren Born New York 1830; graduated from the U.S. Military Academy second in his class in 1850; brevet 2d lieutenant Topographical Engineers; promoted to 2d lieutenant in 1854 and to 1st lieutenant in 1856. Before the Civil War, he surveyed the Mississippi River Delta, supervised river and canal improvements, compiled maps and reports of the Pacific Railroad exploration, served as chief engineer of the Sioux Expedition where he fought Indians and made maps in Dakota and Nebraska territories; taught mathematics at West Point.

In 1861 appointed lieutenant colonel 5th New York Volunteer Infantry, he saw action at Big Bethel and was then promoted to colonel of his regiment and to captain of topographical engineers; in 1862 participated in the Peninsular Campaign and the Battle of the Seven Days, where he was wounded at Gaines' Mill and brevetted lieutenant colonel, U.S. Army, for gallantry; served in the battles of Second Bull Run, Antietam, Centreville, and Fredericksburg; promoted to brigadier general, U.S. Volunteers; in 1863 promoted to major general, U.S. Volunteers, and transferred to regular army engineers; named chief engineer for the Army of the Potomac and married Emily Forbes Chase of Baltimore, with whom he had a son and a daughter; wounded at Gettysburg, where he distinguished himself at Little Round Top and received a brevet promotion to colonel, U.S. Army, for his gallant conduct; commanding the Second Corps from August 1863 to March 1864, he participated in a number of engagements, notably that at Bristoe Station, for which he was brevetted brigadier general and later major general, U.S. Army. Warren commanded the Fifth Corps in actions from the Wilderness to Five Forks, where General Philip H. Sheridan, with Grant's approval, removed him from command for alleged slowness in carrying out orders; Warren resigned from the volunteer service in 1865, but remained in the regular army as major until his promotion to lieutenant colonel engineers in 1879; after repeated requests, fourteen years after the war, he received a court of inquiry that exonerated him of Sheridan's charges. His career shattered by these charges, Warren "died of a broken heart" at Newport, Rhode Island, in 1882.

General John Sedgwick Born Connecticut 1813; received his early education in the Connecticut common schools and spent a few months at an academy; taught school before entering the U.S. Military Academy, from which he graduated twenty-fourth in his class in 1837; appointed 2d lieutenant in the 2d Artillery in 1837; promoted to 1st lieutenant in 1839. Participated in the Seminole War, assisted in moving the Cherokee Indians west of the Mississippi, served on the northern frontier during the Canadian border disturbances, and on various

garrison assignments; participated in the Mexican War; brevetted captain for gallant conduct in the battles of Contreras and Churubusco and major for gallant conduct in the action at Chapultepec; promoted to captain in 1849; after several years of garrison duty, he welcomed his appointment as major in the newly organized 1st Cavalry in 1855; participated in the Utah Expedition of 1857–58, and in the warfare with the Kiowa and Comanche Indians in 1858–60. In 1861 he enjoyed quick promotions to lieutenant colonel of the 2d Cavalry, colonel of the 1st Cavalry, colonel of the 4th Cavalry, and finally brigadier general of volunteers; important assignments followed as brigade and then division commander in the Army of the Potomac; in 1862 he participated in most of the Peninsular Campaign, including Glendale where he was severely wounded; promoted to major general of volunteers in July 1862, he played a prominent role in the Battle of Antietam, where he was again wounded; he commanded for a time the Sixth Corps and the Ninth Corps, but in 1863 he led the Sixth Corps in the Chancellorsville, Fredericksburg, Salem Heights, Gettysburg, Rappahannock Station, and Mine Run operations. In 1864, still commanding the Sixth Corps, he fought in the Wilderness and was killed by a Confederate sniper while directing the placing of artillery at Spotsylvania. Much loved by his men, this strict disciplinarian, a generous and affable bachelor, known to his troops as "Uncle John," was an able corps commander. He is buried in his native town, Cornwall Hollow, Connecticut.

General Winfield Scott Hancock Born Pennsylvania 1824; attended Norristown Academy; graduated from U.S. Military Academy eighteenth in the class of 1844; brevet 2d lieutenant 6th Infantry 1844; 2d lieutenant 1846; participated in Mexican War; brevetted 1st lieutenant 1847 for gallant conduct in the battles of Contreras and Churubusco; following the Mexican War, he spent years as regimental quartermaster and adjutant in Florida, Kansas, Utah, and on the Pacific coast; in 1850 married Almira Russell, daughter of a St. Louis merchant. Promoted to 1st lieutenant 1853; captain in 1855. Appointed brigadier general of volunteers in 1861; prominent in Peninsular Campaign; commanded a division at Antietam; major general volunteers 1862 to 1866; participated in battles of Fredericksburg and Chancellorsville; commanded the Second Corps at Gettysburg, where he achieved lasting fame and the thanks of Congress for turning back the Confederates from the Federal left and center. Hancock never fully recovered from the wound he received at Gettysburg, but commanded his corps in battles from the Wilderness to Appomattox; appointed brigadier general U.S. Army in 1864 for distinguished services; brevetted major general in 1865 for gallant conduct at Spotsylvania. Promoted to major general U.S. Army in 1866; led expedition against hostile Indians in 1867 while commanding the Central Military Department; commanded the Department of Louisiana and Texas in 1867 until Congress removed him for giving civil authorities jurisdiction over all crimes not involving forcible resistance to Federal authority; commanded the Department of Dakota from 1870 to 1872, the Division of  the Atlantic from 1872 to 1876, and finally the Department of the East from 1877 to 1886; presidential candidate of the Democratic party in 1880; died at Governors Island, New York, in 1886. A biographer emphasized Hancock's "great industry, courage, ambition, lofty ideals, [and] unfaltering loyalty to friends." General Grant, noting that Hancock never "committed in battle a blunder," praised his "personal courage" and called him "the most conspicuous figure of all the general officers who did not exercise a separate command."

Winfield Scott Hancock's Second Corps, most of the Yankee cavalry, and the long army supply train crossed the river at Ely's Ford.

Of the nearly 120,000 men under his command, Grant kept only General Ambrose Burnside's independent Ninth Corps north of the river to protect the railroad to Washington. At the river fords and in the Wilderness, Confederate opposition was so light Grant informed the War Department that he would know within the next forty-eight hours "whether the enemy intends giving battle this side of Richmond."

"Gleaming Skulls and Whitish Bones"

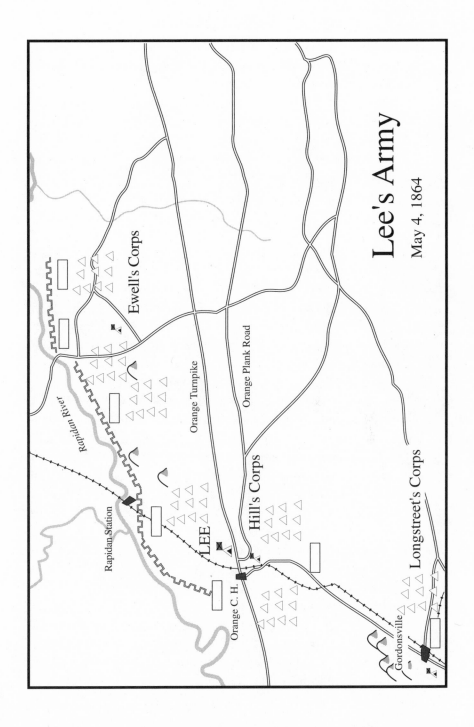

Lee's Army

May 4, 1864

Ewell's Corps

Orange Turnpike

Orange Plank Road

Rapidan River

Rapidan Station

LEE

Orange C. H.

Hill's Corps

Longstreet's Corps

Gordonsville

Soon, however, the whole Union advance bogged down. Grant had expected his army to be near the eastern edge of the Wilderness by nightfall on May 4, but the narrow roads slowed the long lines of men and wagons. As night fell, Warren's and Sedgwick's men were strung out along the Germanna Road and Hancock's Corps was deployed near Chancellorsville, where the terrain provided an eerie setting for the night's bivouac.

Many soldiers found partially buried skeletons, which unnerved veteran and recruit alike. "We wandered to and fro," recalled one man, "looking at the gleaming skulls and whitish bones, and examining the exposed clothing of the dead to see if they had been Union or Confederate soldiers." This ghostly camp site gave soldiers "a sense of ominous dread." An anxious Federal wrote: "[General Joseph] Hooker has been strongly censured for allowing himself to be shut up here in the Wilderness [and defeated by Lee in 1863]. Is Grant to repeat this stupendous piece of folly?"

Meanwhile, Lee scrambled to counter the Union advance. He had hoped to attack the marching columns of Federals as they entered the Wilderness, but Grant's move caught the Confederates still unprepared. During the winter, Lee had been compelled to scatter his army in order to feed it; now, as the Federals moved southward, only two of Lee's three army corps—General Richard S. Ewell's and General A. P. Hill's— were at hand. Longstreet's Corps was forty miles away at Gordonsville and thus out of supporting distance. Moreover, Lee's cavalry commander, General J. E. B. Stuart, who should have been scouting the line of the Rapidan, was still near Fredericksburg. Such a divided army might have given a less bold commander reason to hesitate, but not Lee. When he learned during the night of May 4 that the Federals were still in the Wilderness he at once decided to attack them. After informing Longstreet, and getting "Old Pete's" promise to get his command up in time for battle, Lee ordered Ewell's and

General James Ewell Brown Stuart Born Virginia 1833; of Scotch-Irish and Welsh ancestry, "Jeb" Stuart attended Emory and Henry College 1848–50; graduated thirteenth in the class of 1854 at the U.S. Military Academy; and distinguished himself at West Point by his "almost thankful acceptance" of every offer to fight, although often beaten. Appointed 2d lieutenant in 1st Cavalry and served for six years on the Indian frontier, where he was wounded; promoted to 1st lieutenant in 1855; married Flora, daughter of Colonel Philip St. George Cooke. In 1859, while on leave, he served as Colonel Robert E. Lee's aide in suppressing John Brown's slave rebellion at Harpers Ferry, Va.; promoted to captain in 1861 less than a month before he resigned from the U.S. Army to join the Confederacy; in 1861 he commanded the 1st Virginia Cavalry at First Manassas and later received promotion to brigadier general; in 1862 he commanded the cavalry during the Peninsular Campaign; executed his first "ride around McClellan," ascertaining the Federal army's exact location; screened the left flank of Lee's army during the Seven Days' Battle. Promoted to major general and given command of Lee's cavalry just prior to the Second Manassas

Campaign, Stuart led several raids against Federal forces; participated in the Antietam Campaign, making another spectacular ride around McClellan's army, and commanded his cavalry division at Fredericksburg; in 1863 he temporarily commanded Jackson's Corps at Chancellorsville, after Stonewall and A. P. Hill had been wounded; directed cavalry actions at Brandy Station, the largest and "first true cavalry combat" of the war; conducted a raid during the Gettysburg Campaign for which he received severe criticism; after fighting in the Wilderness and at Spotsylvania, Stuart received a mortal wound at Yellow Tavern on May 11, 1864, and died the next day. He dressed dramatically, with a peacock's plume in his hat and a red flower or a ribbon in his lapel, rode splendid horses, and wore a massive and flowing beard to hide his receding chin, which won him the nickname "Beauty" at West Point. He loved music, dancing, pretty girls, and much jollity, but disallowed drinking or swearing in his presence. Scholars acknowledge Stuart's vanity and exhibitionism along with his bravery, endurance, good humor, and greatness as a cavalryman. Lee, who considered Stuart "the eyes of his army," said of him: "He never brought me a piece of false information."

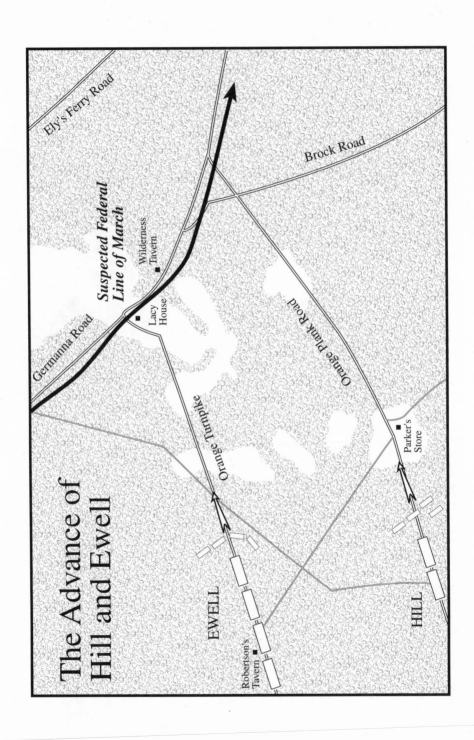

The Advance of Hill and Ewell

Hill's corps to move into the Wilderness on the morning of May 5. Ewell marched along the Turnpike, now State Route 20, the northernmost route toward Fredericksburg, while Hill, with Lee leading the column, took the parallel Plank Road, now State Route 621, farther south. Lee expected that his line of march would put Ewell's and Hill's men in position to attack Grant's exposed right flank, but he wanted no major battle until Longstreet got there with the remaining third of the army. Confident that Grant's large force would be less formidable in the Wilderness, Lee expected to have about 62,000 men when Longstreet arrived.

The first clash of forces, on the morning of May 5, surprised both sides. Ewell, advancing eastward along the Turnpike, collided with Warren, who was marching southward on the Germanna Road. Lee, still waiting for Longstreet, insisted on no general engagement yet; the Federals, on the other hand, simply wanted to get out of the Wilderness.

Partly because the Wilderness was a nightmare for horsemen, the cavalry of both armies had done their work so poorly that neither commander knew the other's exact location or strength. Meade thought that Warren had met a delaying force, perhaps a division, left behind by Lee to cover a Confederate concentration farther south along the North Anna River. Uncertain just what Warren faced, Meade ordered Sedgwick to cover Warren's right flank and Hancock to halt his march southward until Warren could determine the actual strength of the Confederates he had encountered.

Warren, following Meade's orders, advanced against the Confederates. But soon the Federals became tangled in the underbrush. "We fought them with bayonet as well as bullet," remembered a Union officer. "Up through the trees rolled dense clouds of battle smoke, circling about the pines and mingling with the flowering dogwoods. Each man fought on his own, grimly and desperately." Ewell counterattacked, turned

General Richard S. Ewell Born D.C. (of Virginian stock) 1817; graduated U.S. Military Academy in 1840, thirteenth in his class; appointed 2d lieutenant in the 1st Dragoons; promoted to 1st lieutenant in 1845; served on the frontier; participated in the Mexican War; brevetted captain in 1847 for gallant conduct at Contreras and Churubusco; promoted to captain in 1849; won further distinction against the Apaches in New Mexico in 1857. Resigned from U.S. Army in 1861 to join the

Confederacy; appointed lieutenant colonel of cavalry and wounded at Fairfax Court House, Va., in June, he quickly advanced to brigadier general and command of a brigade at the First Battle of Manassas; promoted to major general in 1862, Ewell led a division in the Shenandoah Valley under Stonewall Jackson's command at Winchester and Cross Keys; fought next at Gaines' Mill in defense of Richmond, and then during the Second Manassas Campaign at Cedar Mountain and Groveton, where he received a wound that cost him his left leg. Recuperated under the care of his first cousin, Lizinka Campbell Brown, whom he married in May 1863; promoted to lieutenant general and given command of a corps after Stonewall Jackson's death, Ewell defeated a large Federal force at Winchester, led the Army of Northern Virginia's advance into Pennsylvania, and launched an attack on the Federal right at Gettysburg, but failed to take Cemetery Ridge, for which he received considerable criticism. In 1864 he commanded his corps in the Wilderness and at Spotsylvania, but Ewell's broken health forced Lee to transfer him from corps command to responsibility for the defense of Richmond; in 1865, during the retreat toward Appomattox, Ewell commanded a mixed corps of soldiers, sailors, and marines; surrounded and forced to surrender at Sayler's Creek, he was imprisoned until summer; moved to his wife's plantation in Maury County, Tennessee, where he died of pneumonia on January 25, 1872, just five days after his wife succumbed to the same illness. Douglas S. Freeman described him as "bald, pop-eyed and long beaked, with a piping voice that seems to fit his appearance as a strange, unlovely bird"; his sharp tongue matched his fighting spirit, but the loss of his leg, headaches, indigestion, and sleeplessness drained both his energy and effectiveness. "A truer and nobler spirit never drew sword," proclaimed General Longstreet.

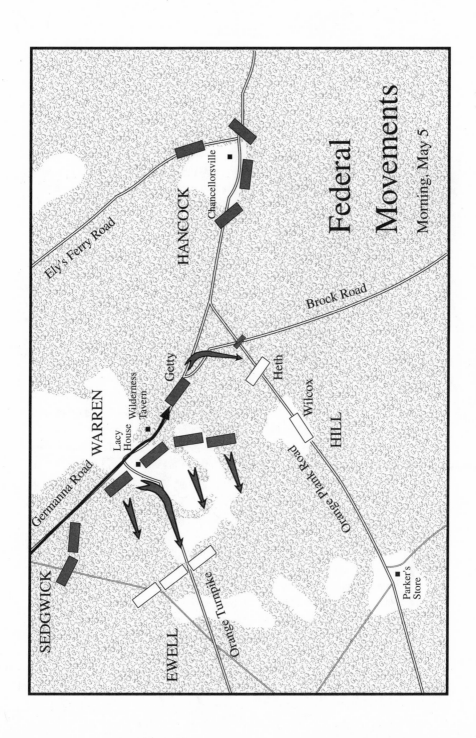

Federal Movements

Morning, May 5

General Ambrose Powell Hill Born Virginia 1825; graduated fifteenth in the class of 1847 at the U.S. Military Academy; 2d lieutenant 1st Artillery in 1847 and served in Mexico, but saw no action; 1st lieutenant in 1851; participated in Florida Seminole campaigns; served in D.C. office of coast survey, 1855 to 1860; married Kitty Morgan McClung, sister of John Hunt Morgan, in 1859. Resigned from U.S. Army in 1861; appointed colonel of 13th Virginia Infantry; in 1862 promoted to

brigadier general; commanded brigade and won praise at Williamsburg; promoted to major general and given command of the Confederacy's largest division, which he led successfully but with heavy losses during the Battle of the Seven Days. Transferred after a disagreement with Longstreet to Stonewall Jackson's command, Hill received praise for his actions at Cedar Mountain and Second Manassas, yet enjoyed his greatest fame for saving the Army of Northern Virginia from defeat by his timely arrival on Lee's right flank at Antietam; in December 1862 his careless posting of troops at Fredericksburg heightened a controversy between Hill and Jackson that ended only with Stonewall's death following the Battle of Chancellorsville in May 1863. Promoted to lieutenant general and given command of the newly formed Third Corps in Lee's army, Hill opened the Battle of Gettysburg, but sickness limited his effectiveness; he repulsed Federals at Falling Waters, on the retreat to Virginia, but suffered his worst defeat making a bold attack at Bristoe Station in October. In 1864 he fought in the Wilderness, but illness deprived him of command from May 8 to 21. Participated in actions from the North Anna River to Cold Harbor, and in Lee's defense of Petersburg, where from June 1864 to March 1865 Hill met and defeated "every Federal effort to break Lee's right"; late in March he took sick leave, suffering, his best biographer explains, from kidney malfunctions that slowly produced uremia, the results of a gonorrhea infection contracted during a summer 1844 furlough from West Point; Hill returned to the front on April 2, 1865, where he was killed trying to reestablish his lines. Genial but quarrelsome, reckless and impetuous in battle, tall, thin, and weighing just 145 pounds, "Little Powell" favored bright red shirts and enjoyed the confidence of his troops. "A more brilliant, useful soldier and chivalrous gentleman never adorned the Confederate army," said General William Mahone.

General George Washington Getty Born Georgetown, D.C., 1819; graduated fifteenth in his class at the U.S. Military Academy in 1840; appointed 2d lieutenant in the 4th Artillery in 1840; promoted to 1st lieutenant in 1845; served in the Mexican War; brevetted captain in 1847 for gallant conduct in the battles of Contreras and Churubusco; in 1848 he married Elizabeth Graham Stevenson; in 1849–50 and in 1856–57 he fought against the Seminoles in Florida; in 1853 promoted to captain. In 1861 transferred to the 5th Artillery; in 1862 he commanded four batteries at Yorktown, Gaines' Mill, and Malvern Hill; he also fought at South Mountain and Antietam; appointed brigadier general of volunteers in 1862, he commanded a division in the Ninth Corps at Fredericksburg; assigned command of a division at Suffolk, Va., that protected the approach to Norfolk and Hampton Roads from the south; successfully defended Suffolk from Confederate attack, personally leading a storming column that captured Battery Huger; in the summer of 1863 he led an expedition to the South Anna River. In 1864 he commanded the Second Division, Sixth Corps, in the Wilderness where he was severely wounded. Participated in the siege of Petersburg until Grant detached the Sixth and Nineteenth corps to protect Washington from Jubal Early's threat; after that danger ended, the Sixth Corps became part of Sheridan's army operating in the Shenandoah Valley; Getty commanded his division and occasionally the Sixth Corps throughout the

campaign, fighting at Winchester, Fisher's Hill, and Cedar Creek; he participated in the final operations of the Army of the Potomac around Petersburg and in the pursuit of Lee's army to Appomattox; brevetted for gallant conduct and for his war service, he remained in the regular army after the war. Became colonel of the 27th Infantry in 1866; transferred to 3rd Infantry in 1869; transferred to 3rd Artillery in 1870; member of the board that reversed Fitz-John Porter's court martial in 1878–79; transferred to 4th Artillery in 1882; retired in 1883; lived the remainder of his life on a farm near Forest Glen, Maryland; died in 1901. Getty was a courteous, modest, and distinguished soldier.

the Federal flank, and forced Warren back. After retaking the ground the Confederates had lost, Ewell entrenched.

The next encounter occurred near the intersection of the Brock Road and the Plank Road, along which Lee advanced with Hill's Corps. That action began when some Federal cavalrymen dismounted and used their repeating carbines to

General Henry Heth Born Virginia 1825; graduated in 1847 from the U.S. Military Academy at the bottom of his class of thirty-eight students; appointed brevet 2d lieutenant in 1st Infantry in 1847; promoted to 2d lieutenant in 6th Infantry in 1847 and to 1st lieutenant in 1853; married his first cousin, Harriet Selden. Served as regimental quartermaster, 1854 to 1855; promoted to captain in the 10th Infantry in 1855. Spent his antebellum career on the frontier; resigned from U.S. Army in

1861; organized the 45th Virginia Infantry and became its colonel in 1861; promoted to brigadier general in 1862 and sent to western Virginia where he suffered defeat at Lewisburg; served with General E. Kirby Smith in the invasion of Kentucky; transferred to Army of Northern Virginia in 1863; wounded at Chancellorsville where he commanded a brigade; promoted to major general and given command of a division; precipitated the Battle of Gettysburg, where his division suffered heavy losses and a bullet penetrated his padded hat, cracked his skull, and incapacitated him for the remaining action at Gettysburg; badly defeated at Falling Creek, during the retreat into Virginia. In 1864 at the Wilderness, he fought his old friend General Hancock; at Spotsylvania, Heth's horse was shot from under him; commanded his division in battles south to Petersburg; carrying a battle flag, he led his men in capturing the Union position at Reams' Station; surrendered what remained of his division at Appomattox. After the war, he failed at various business ventures; served for a time with the Bureau of Indian Affairs, wrote his memoirs, and died of Bright's disease in 1899. Courteous, handsome, and brave, Heth was solidly reliable but only a mediocre division commander.

General Cadmus Marcellus Wilcox Born North Carolina 1824; moved with his family to Tennessee; attended the University of Nashville; graduated from the U.S. Military Academy fifty-fourth in his class in 1846; brevetted 2d lieutenant in 4th Infantry in 1846; promoted to 2d lieutenant in the 7th Infantry in 1847. Served with both Taylor and Scott in the Mexican War; brevetted 1st lieutenant for gallant conduct in the Battle of Chapultepec; promoted to 1st lieutenant in 1851; taught tactics at West Point; visited Europe; published *Rifles and Rifle Practice* in 1859; promoted to captain in 1860. Resigned from U.S. Army in 1861; appointed colonel of the 9th Alabama Infantry; present at First Manassas; promoted to brigadier general in October 1861; in 1862 he fought at Williamsburg, Seven Pines, and the Seven Days' Battle, where his brigade lost 1,055 of its 1,800 men, and thereafter he was with Lee's army in nearly every major battle; during the summer of 1862 he commanded three brigades, but failed to receive promotion to division command because of lack of support from General Longstreet, whom Wilcox loathed. His greatest service came during the Chancellorsville Campaign in May 1863 when he stopped the Federal advance near Salem Church; after Gettysburg, he was promoted to major general and given command of a division; in 1864 he fought well in the Wilderness and at Spotsylvania, and remained steady during the

withdrawal southward to Petersburg; more than once his division suffered heavy losses, but negligence was never suggested; during negotiations at Appomattox, several Union generals sought to find and take their old friend Wilcox to visit Grant. After the war, Wilcox, a bachelor, lived in Washington with the widow and two children of his elder brother; he refused commissions in the Egyptian and Korean armies; in 1886 President Cleveland appointed him chief of the railroad division of the General Land Office, a position he held until his death in 1890. After his death his niece edited and published in 1892 his *History of the Mexican War.* General Henry Heth said of Wilcox: "I know of no man of rank on the Southern side who had more warm friends, *North and South.*"

slow Hill's march. Meade had no idea how many Confederates threatened the road junction, but he realized the importance of holding the Brock Road; if it was lost, Hancock's Corps and most of the Federal cavalry would be separated from the rest of the army.

As soon as he heard of the skirmishing, therefore, he sent General George Washington Getty's Division from Sedgwick's Corps to hold the crossroads until Hancock could bring up his corps. Getty arrived before noon and learned from captured Confederates that he faced two of Hill's divisions, those of Henry Heth and Cadmus Marcellus Wilcox. Getty, a Mexican War veteran and a West Point classmate of Sherman and Ewell, decided to construct light entrenchments near the crossroads while awaiting the arrival of Hancock's troops.

4

"Let the Men Rest"

These opening encounters had been fought blindly and with much confusion. Soldiers on both sides had stumbled toward each other through the brambles and thick growth. Numbers meant little; indeed, in the Wilderness, with vision limited by the thickness of the woods, officers lost control of their commands. Attackers thrashed noisily through the underbrush, perfect targets for concealed defenders. During attacks and retreats, formations and alignments disintegrated. Fighting in this dense forest, the Confederates enjoyed two great advantages: they were, on the whole, better woodsmen than their opponents and they were far more familiar with the terrain.

Neither side seemed in a hurry to renew the fighting. The positions of Ewell and Warren, facing each other along the Turnpike, remained relatively stable. Farther south, Hancock's

Corps began arriving at the junction of the Brock and Plank roads shortly after 2 P.M., but the men did not go directly into battle. As the units came up they formed on Getty's left flank and rear. Hancock, told that the Confederates were expected to attack, ordered his troops to throw up light breastworks.

General Lee, still waiting for Longstreet, was in no rush. He sat on a shady lawn at the Widow Tapp's farm casually conversing with some of his officers, including Generals Stuart and Hill, when a regiment of Union troops emerged from the woods. But instead of charging forward and capturing the

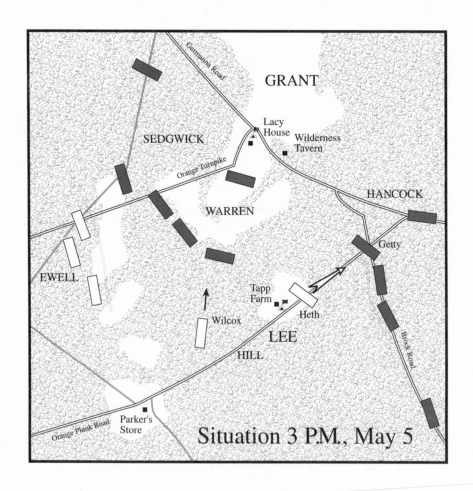

Situation 3 P.M., May 5

startled Confederates, the Federals turned around and marched back into the forest. This was as close as Lee came to being captured during the war. Realizing that the Federals were closer than he had expected, Lee quickly developed two plans: to seize the Brock Road without bringing on a major engagement and to link Hill's units with Ewell's. After sending Wilcox's Division northward to extend a thin line of Confederates from the Plank Road to the Turnpike, Lee ordered Heth's Division to advance toward the Brock Road.

As the Confederates moved forward, the Federals attacked. Just after 4 P.M. Hancock received orders from Meade directing "that Getty attack at once, and that you support him with your whole corps." The staff officer who delivered this order wrote his wife: "At the crossroad sat Hancock, on his fine horse—the preux chevalier of this campaign—a glorious soldier, indeed! The musketry was crashing in the woods in our front, and stray balls—too many to be pleasant—were coming about. It's all very well for novels, but I don't like such places and go there only when ordered."

The fighting took place in the Wilderness's thickest brush. "The scrubby woods and tangled thickets stretch away on every side, interminably to all appearance," noted an officer. "The narrow roads offer the only means of going anywhere or of seeing anything. Once off, then low ridges and hollows succeed each other, without a single feature to serve as a landmark, and no one but an experienced woodsman with a compass could keep his bearings and position or preserve his course." In such terrain Heth's 6,700 Confederates faced the onslaught of some 30,000 Federals, Hancock's Corps plus Getty's Division.

"Nothing could be seen except trees and brush," reported a Union soldier. "All we could see of the enemy was the flash of their guns. This was guide enough, and we blazed away at them." But the Federals had difficulty using their numerical

superiority. An officer confessed: "It was difficult to tell who
was who; our division and [another unit] became sandwiched
in a most remarkable manner. We saw the most awful
confusion. Numerical superiority was at its worst. There were
more troops than could be utilized, almost a huddle. The roads
were narrow and the woods and underbrush very dense. It was
a dreadfully mixed-up mess."

Even so, the Federals forced the Confederates back. "From
4 o'clock on we were into it all along the line, hot and heavy,

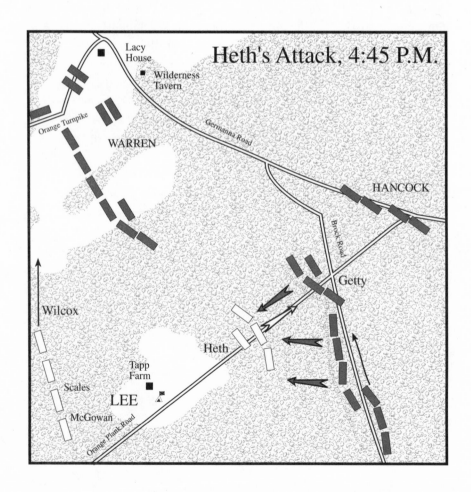

teeth and nails, nip and tuck," wrote a Maine volunteer. "It was a continuous roar of musketry, rising and swelling like the sound of surf pounding on the shore." As Heth's men retreated, Lee had to recall Wilcox's Division and abandon any attempt to link up with Ewell.

Wilcox's men, especially two Carolina brigades, arrived just in time to prevent the collapse of Heth's left. In their counterattack against the oncoming Yankees, General Alfred M. Scales's North Carolinians took heavy casualties. After

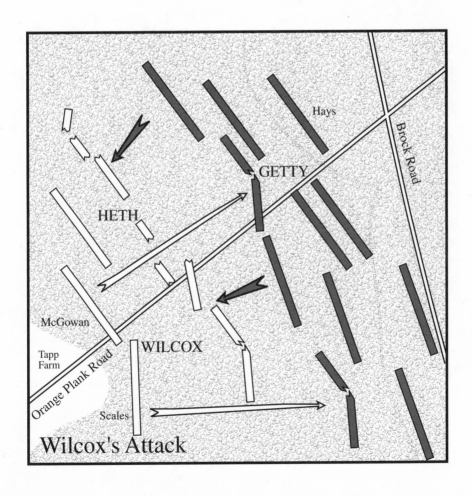

Wilcox's Attack

General Alfred Moore Scales Born North Carolina 1827; served in the state legislature and one term in Congress, 1857–59. A secessionist in 1861, he enlisted as a private in the Rockingham Guards, which became Company H, 3d North Carolina Infantry; elected captain of his company and then colonel of the regiment, which was redesignated the 13th North Carolina Infantry; in 1862 Scales and his regiment engaged in a rare bayonet fight at Williamsburg, where three of his companies were "nearly annihilated"; they next fought at Seven Pines and then,

transferred to Samuel Garland's Brigade, fought hard in the Seven Days' Battle, where Garland called Scales "conspicuous for his fine bearing," seizing "the colors at a critical moment and advancing to the front." Following the fighting on the Peninsula, Scales collapsed from exhaustion, and "lay ill, nigh unto death" for several weeks; he fought next at Fredericksburg in December, temporarily commanding the brigade of William Dorsey Pender, an old friend who had been slightly wounded. In 1863 Scales took leave to marry a young woman half his age, but returned to fight at Chancellorsville, where his regiment captured Union General William Hays and Scales received a thigh wound that disabled him for several weeks; promoted to brigadier general, he returned to action at Gettysburg, losing all but one of his field officers and suffering a severe leg wound; he recuperated and resumed command in August, but saw little action during the remainder of the year. In 1864 he fought fiercely at the Wilderness— where his old regiment lost its flag—at Spotsylvania, and on the way to Petersburg, except at North Anna, where illness incapacitated him; he led his brigade during the Petersburg siege, but Scales was in North Carolina on sick leave when his men surrendered at Appomattox. After the war he served his state as congressman, 1875–84, and governor, 1884–88; he died in 1892. An admirer described Scales as efficient, capable, and brave, with a calmness and coolness that made him a skillful brigade commander.

seeing three successive color bearers shot down, a captain in the 22d North Carolina Regiment grabbed a flag and rushed toward the enemy, hollering, "Follow me!" At the end of the action, when the Federals had been driven back, General Scales embraced the captain: "God bless you! I saw your conduct with that flag! You have saved the army!"

General Samuel McGowan's Brigade, composed of five South Carolina regiments, would hit the Yankees even harder. A day before, orders to march had disrupted their cooking, but within thirty minutes these regiments broke camp, packed knapsacks and rolled blankets, thrust half-raw rations into haversacks, threw aside nine months' accumulated plunder, and marched eastward with other units of Hill's Corps.

Late on the afternoon of May 5, as the brigade passed near General Lee, "a rambling skirmish fire" could be heard. Soon the brigade halted on what one officer called "a clear, commanding ridge. It was one of the most impressive scenes I ever witnessed." On his left, looking north, he could see in the distance Ewell's Corps engaging the Federals. To his right "the sharp crack of rifles gradually swelled; above was [sic] the blue, placid heavens; around us a varied landscape of forest and fields, green with the earliest foliage of spring; and here knelt hirsute and browned veterans striving for another struggle with death." Chaplain Francis Patrick Mullally of Orr's South Carolina Rifles, a Presbyterian native of Tipperary who left Ireland after participating in an insurrection against the English, led the men in prayer until "the roar of muskets became continuous."

Ordered to advance "through the thick undergrowth," McGowan's Brigade moved to reinforce Heth's Division, "now much thinned and exhausted. We had very imprudently begun to cheer," noted an officer. "We passed over [Heth's] line cheering. There was no use of this. We should have charged

General Samuel McGowan Born South Carolina 1819; son of Irish Presbyterian immigrants; graduated from South Carolina College in 1841; studied law in Abbeville under T. C. Perrin; admitted to the bar in 1842; reprimanded John Cunningham, an experienced duelist, for uncomplimentary remarks about a young woman, accepted Cunningham's challenge, and received a slight wound in the duel that followed; became Perrin's law partner, a popular politician, and an eloquent advocate; elected major general in the state militia and represented

Abbeville District in the state legislature; married Susan Caroline Wardlaw, daughter of distinguished Abbeville Judge David L. Wardlaw. In 1846 McGowan enlisted as a private in the famous Palmetto Regiment for service in the Mexican War; rose to the rank of captain and received praise for his gallant conduct in storming Chapultepec; in 1861, as a brigade commander, he assisted in the capture of Fort Sumter; in 1862 became colonel of the 14th South Carolina Infantry in Maxcy Gregg's Brigade; given brigade command and promoted to brigadier general after Gregg's death in 1863; McGowan served in that capacity displaying extraordinary bravery until the surrender at Appomattox; wounded four times—at Gaines' Mill, Second Manassas, Chancellorsville, and Spotsylvania. After the war, he resumed the practice of law in Abbeville; in 1865 he served as a member of the state constitutional convention and was elected to Congress, but the Republican majority denied him his seat; involved in the struggle to redeem South Carolina from Republican rule in 1876; elected to the state legislature in 1878 and a year later made an associate justice of the South Carolina Supreme Court; defeated for reelection by forces of Ben Tillman, whom McGowan had antagonized by casting the deciding Supreme Court vote declaring the proposed liquor dispensary unconstitutional; died at his home in Abbeville in 1897. Commanding in appearance, courageous, and full of simple humor, McGowan was one of the best regimental and brigade commanders in the Army of Northern Virginia.

without uttering a word until within a few yards of the Federal line. As it was, we drew upon ourselves a terrific volley of musketry."

The South Carolinians "swept through the Wilderness like a tornado, driving everything before it," reported General Wilcox. Not only did McGowan's men capture hundreds of Getty's troops; they forced one Federal unit to break "in a disgraceful manner."

Soon McGowan's men fought themselves into trouble. Their advance, which outran any support, had been impeded from the outset by the matted wilderness growth of saplings and bushes. Outnumbered by the Federals and trying to advance over "the worst conceivable ground for marching," the South Carolinians realized that Heth's Division, through which they had just passed, was now firing through their ranks at the enemy. Regiments became separated; men pushed ahead until they lost connection with the rest of the brigade and found themselves surrounded by the Federals. "All idea of [continuing our] charge had to be abandoned," lamented an officer, and finally Federal fire became so severe that General McGowan ended his advance and withdrew a short distance to the rear.

New Federal attacks followed, but the Confederate lines held. "It was a fearful experience," remembered a Union officer, and another Federal testified: "There are but one or two square miles upon this continent that have been more saturated with blood." Every Union assault, remembered a Massachusetts chaplain, "was mowed down by bullets from unseen lines of musketry." At 6 P.M. the Yankees still assaulted Heth's battered lines while a member of Lee's staff quietly prayed, "If night would only come."

By late afternoon Hays's Brigade had joined the Federal advance. Its commander, General Alexander Hays, appeared to be a rough sort of man, "the epitome of a brigade commander," but his men knew he had a warm heart. A personal friend of both Grant and Hancock, whom he had known at West Point and served with in Mexico, Hays rode with his staff along the lines as his brigade deployed. Encountering his old regiment, he stopped briefly to encourage the men of the 63rd Pennsylvania. Just then Hays reeled from a bullet wound in the head, fell from his saddle, and died within a few hours. That morning, in his last letter to his wife, Hays had spoken

General Alexander Hays Born Pennsylvania 1819; attended Allegheny College; graduated U.S. Military Academy twentieth in his class in 1844; brevetted 2d lieutenant in 4th Infantry in 1844; promoted to 2d lieutenant in the 8th Infantry in 1846; married Annie Adams McFadden. Served on the frontier and in the Mexican

War; brevetted first lieutenant in 1846 for gallant conduct in the battles of Palo Alto and Resaca de la Palma; resigned from the U.S. Army in 1848; engaged in the iron industry but with little success; after failing to find gold in California in 1849, Hays returned to Pennsylvania; after 1851 engaged in engineering and construction work. At outbreak of Civil War, he returned to the army as captain in the 16th Infantry, but soon became colonel of the 63rd Pennsylvania Volunteers; promoted to brigadier general of volunteers in 1862, Hays fought gallantly at Fair Oaks, the Peach Orchard, Glendale, and Malvern Hill, for which he received regular army brevet promotions to major and lieutenant colonel; severely wounded in the Battle of Second Manassas; in 1863 given command of a division in the Army of the Potomac; brevetted colonel for his conduct at Gettysburg, and served successively in the pursuit to Warrenton and in the Rapidan Campaign; killed in action on the second day of the Battle of the Wilderness; posthumously promoted to brevet major general of volunteers for his gallant conduct during fighting on the Peninsula, at Gettysburg, and in the Wilderness. His rigorous orders to his troops to refrain from violence against civilians in enemy territory revealed his character. "God help the violator," Hays said, "so long as I command." Grant wrote, "With him it was 'Come, boys,' not 'Go.'"

of death: "This beautiful [morning] might have been an appropriate harbinger of the day of the regeneration of mankind; but it only brought to remembrance, through the throats of many bugles, that duty enjoined upon each one, perhaps, before the setting sun, to lay down a life for his country."

Both sides were exhausted, but in the growing darkness, just after 7 P.M., Hill learned that a Federal division was moving into the gap between him and Ewell. Hill had no

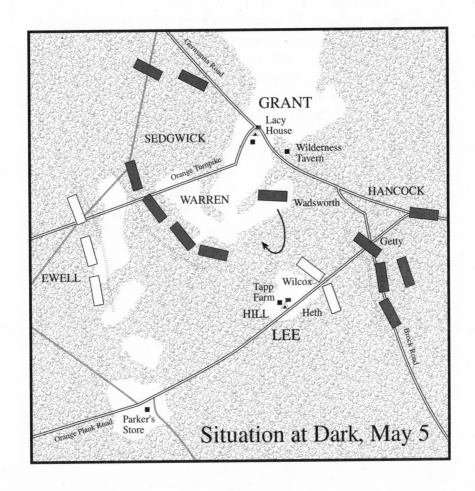

Situation at Dark, May 5

reserves; to withdraw a single regiment from his battle line might bring disaster. His only available troops were 125 Alabamians who were guarding prisoners. Hill placed them in a skirmish line, told them to charge through the woods screaming the rebel yell, and hoped they might fool the Yankees into thinking the attackers were the lead elements of several Confederate brigades. The noisy charge through the woods by the Alabamians so unnerved General James S. Wadsworth's Division that it halted for the night and threw up earthworks.

General Lee, who knew how close his men had been to being driven from the field, let Hill's battered troops rest for the night where they had fought. Their magnificent stand had left them shaken and somewhat scattered, and well it might have—15,000 of them had held off 40,000 Federals. "Hill did not stand on the defensive but made repeated dashes upon the enemy," recalled an admirer. "He conducted the engagement with great spirit and aggressiveness, repeatedly broke Hancock's line of battle, and compelled him to use his reserves." A North Carolinian, lamenting the killed and wounded, denounced the day's conflict as "butchery pure and simple." The exhausted Confederates, many of them without ammunition, remained disorganized throughout the night. Both Heth and Wilcox urged the ailing Hill to rearrange his lines and to prepare the men for the next day. But Hill replied, "General Lee's orders are to let the men rest as they are." Wilcox went from his conference with Hill to see Lee, who reassured Wilcox that Longstreet "will be up, and the two divisions that have been so actively engaged will be relieved before day."

But the First Corps failed to arrive before daybreak. When Hill awoke around 4 A.M. on May 6 Longstreet's men were not deployed at the front; indeed, they were not near the front. They were still two miles in the rear at Parker's Store, and their absence made Hill's lines dangerously vulnerable. About five o'clock, just after Hill went off to inspect the interval between his left and Ewell's right, Longstreet rode up. Virginia historian Clifford Dowdey blamed the general's lateness on his "congenital slothfulness." Whatever the reason, Hill's chief of staff rushed to shake Longstreet's hand, exclaiming: "Ah, General, we have been looking for you since twelve o'clock last night." Longstreet ignored the remark. "My troops are not up," he began. "I have ridden ahead." At that moment an explosion of musketry along the battle line drowned his voice. The Federals were again attacking.

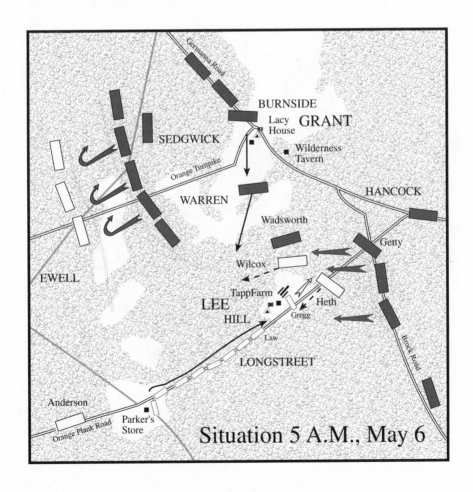

Situation 5 A.M., May 6

Grant, disappointed that Hancock had failed to break Hill's line the day before, hoped that on this day a determined attack by four Federal corps would soundly beat Lee. In addition to directing Hancock, Warren, and Sedgwick to move against the Confederates, Grant also ordered Burnside to advance at 2 A.M. with two divisions to fill the gap between Warren and Hancock. But when the attack started at 5 A.M., Burnside was still trying to find his way through the roadless tangle of undergrowth between the Turnpike and the Plank Road.

The Federal attack achieved varying results. The assault against the Confederates on the Turnpike failed. Ewell

Ewell's Breastworks North of the Turnpike

repulsed Sedgwick and Warren with heavy Union losses. Farther south Hill's men, battered in front and flank by Hancock's massive attack, retreated toward the Tapp farm. By 6 A.M., Hill's situation had changed from dangerous to critical. Lee would report after the battle that the Federal attack "created some confusion." It did much more than that; it nearly drove Hill's Corps from the field.

5

"THOSE MEN ARE NOT WHIPPED"

Confederate officers tried desperately to rally their men. As some veterans rushed past him, Lee shouted: "My God, General McGowan! Is this splendid brigade of yours running like a flock of geese?" "General," replied McGowan, "those men are not whipped! They only want a place to form, and they will fight as well as they ever did!"

Lee, as his troops seemed to melt away, looked again for Longstreet. To General Wilcox, Lee said with anxiety in his voice, "Longstreet must be here! Go bring him!" Wilcox raced up the Plank Road as the Army of Northern Virginia faced its worst crisis since that 1862 afternoon at Antietam.

The Federal advance had now reached the Widow Tapp farm, near Lee's headquarters. "Our troops had moved with wonderful celerity and had turned the Rebs right out of their blankets," noted a Federal. Only a few pieces of Confederate artillery at the edge of a farm clearing stood between the

Federals and victory. These gunners, in fear of hitting Confederate wounded between them and the enemy, held their fire. Afraid that all would be captured if the artillerymen waited any longer, Hill ordered them to disregard the wounded and to fire on the Federals. The guns opened on the oncoming masses, cutting large holes in the Union ranks. A Union officer recalled "the roar of guns" and the effect of canister on his

General John Gregg Born Alabama 1828; attended LaGrange College, taught school, and practiced law in Tuscumbia before moving in 1854 to Texas; settled at Fairfield; married Mary Garth; elected a district judge; an ardent secessionist, he was a member of the convention that voted Texas out of the Union in 1861 and he represented the state in the provisional Congress that met in Montgomery to organize the Confederate government. After fighting began in the summer, Gregg returned to Texas and organized the 7th Texas Infantry, which elected him its colonel; captured in 1862 along with his regiment when Fort Donelson surrendered to General Grant; after spending several months as a prisoner of war before being exchanged in August, Gregg received promotion to brigadier general and command of a brigade composed of Texas and Tennessee troops. Defended Chickasaw Bluffs against Sherman's army in December; sent with his brigade to Port Hudson, La., but in May 1863 moved to join Joseph E. Johnston's forces east of Vicksburg; Gregg's brigade engaged in the action at Jackson before being transferred to the Army of Tennessee; participated in the Battle of  Chickamauga, where he was seriously wounded; when able to return to duty in 1864, he was given command of the Texas Brigade, formerly Hood's Brigade, Army of Northern Virginia. After the Battle of the Wilderness, Gregg and his men fought courageously at Spotsylvania, the North Anna River, Cold Harbor, and in defense of Petersburg; in October 1864 in an attempt to recapture part of the Confederate trenches east of Richmond, Gregg died leading an unsuccessful attack down the Darbytown Road. Brave, capable, and esteemed, Gregg was what one officer called "a born soldier."

men. But the odds were impossible; an artillery battalion was no match for an infantry corps.

Just as the Federals moved to outflank and capture the guns, a handful of Confederates came running eastward down the Plank Road. They were Texans from Hood's old Brigade, now commanded by General John Gregg, the first of Longstreet's men. Lee was so happy to see them that he waved his hat and shouted: "Hurrah for Texas! Hurrah for Texas!" He told Gregg: "When you go in there give those men the cold steel. They will stand and fire all day, and never move unless you charge them." Gregg replied, "That is my experience." Just then, an aide from Longstreet rode up, saying: "Advance your command, General Gregg." Gregg shouted, "Attention, Texas Brigade! The eyes of General Lee are upon you! Forward march!" As the men advanced, Lee said, "Texans always move them!" In response, a weeping soldier cried out between cheers: "I would charge hell itself for that old man."

Lee, captivated by the excitement, lifted his hat and rode forward to lead them. Realizing what he intended, the Texans called out: "Go back, General Lee, go back!" He ignored them, his eyes aflame and fixed on the enemy. A tall sergeant grabbed Lee's bridle rein, but the general continued forward until his aide, Colonel Charles Venable, shouted in Lee's ear for him to turn back and give orders to Longstreet. Lee halted, waved his hat to the onrushing Texans, and then turned his horse and rode back to consult with Longstreet, who bluntly told him that he should go farther behind the lines.

Near the van of Longstreet's forces, Colonel William C. Oates of the 15th Alabama Regiment recalled passing within a few feet of General Lee: "He sat his fine gray horse, 'Traveller,' with the cape of his black cloak around his shoulders, his face flushed and full of animation." Oates remembered bullets "flying around" General Lee, who "had just returned from attempting to lead the Texas Brigade in a charge." Turning calmly, Lee pointed down the road toward the enemy, and asked his chief of staff to "send an active young officer down there." At that moment, Colonel Oates recalled, he considered General Lee "the grandest specimen of manhood I ever beheld. He looked as though he ought to have been, and was, the monarch of the world. He glanced his eye down on the 'ragged rebels' as they filed around him...to their place in line, and inquired: "What troops are these?'" A private answered strongly: "Law's Alabama Brigade." "God bless the Alabamians!" exclaimed General Lee. The men cheered and began their advance with a whoop.

Longstreet had nine fresh brigades to put into the fight. They swept through what was left of Hill's lines and crashed into the Federals. "Like a fine lady at a party," wrote a cannoneer, "Longstreet was often late in his arrival at the ball, but he always made a sensation with the grand old First Corps, sweeping behind him, as his train."

The battle lasted all day, with numerous attacks and counterattacks. Courage meshed with blood and suffering. Half the men in the Texas Brigade (three Texas and one Arkansas regiments) fell in the action, and various units on both sides suffered more than 50 percent casualties. A member of the 11th Alabama Infantry recalled that Longstreet's men "moved forward over the remains of the troops" who had been killed the previous day. "As the Yankees advanced our men poured volley after volley into their lines. Finally they faltered and began to give way; then the yell and charge. We drove them back and recovered all the ground lost the day before."

This veteran especially remembered several sharpshooters standing tall and firing "over our heads." One was his uncle, Joe Shuttlesworth, who "stood up bravely in the rear of his company until he was mortally wounded." As the ambulance corps removed him from the field, one of his litter bearers received a wound and fell, "letting his suffering burden fall to the ground. Sitting on his war horse, Gen. Lee witnessed the incident with manifest tenderness and sympathy. Lifting his hat, Joe said: 'Don't be uneasy. That is the Eleventh Alabama, and they are filling the road with dead Yankees.' Gen. Lee answered: 'I know they are, my brave boy.' Just then the Rebel yell burst forth, and Joe said: 'I told you so.' He died in the hospital that night."

Colonel John M. Stone, commanding Davis's Brigade, retook the position from which he had been driven the day before. Although severely wounded, he refused to leave the field, and burst into tears as he saw the bodies of his fallen comrades about him. After the battle, General Hill rode up and saluted him. "Colonel Stone," he said, "you have won laurels today. I hope soon to see you a major general." The modest Stone replied: "General Hill, I have only done my duty, and if you have any compliments to bestow, give them to these men standing here and their comrades left on the field; they did the fighting, and they deserve the 'laurels.'"

A Georgian had the courage to assist a wounded Union soldier. Shot in the thigh, the man needed help in getting in an upright position behind a tree where he would be in less danger of being hit by his own men. "I gave him the required assistance," recalled the Georgian, who then followed the fight in another direction and never saw the Federal soldier again.

As both sides began to wear down, Meade directed Sedgwick and Warren to stop their attacks on Ewell and to entrench. Meade also sent reinforcements to Hancock, whose troops, having lost their earlier momentum, were falling back to their Brock Road breastworks. Most of Hill's men were back in action, supporting Longstreet's troops who had stormed ahead. "So impetuously was the assault made," admitted a Federal, "that the Union troops melted before it and soon came rolling back, followed by the exultant Confederates." The

Federals continued to fight, remembered a soldier, but they
now battled like a frightened mob with "no organization, no
alignment."

During the late morning, Longstreet received Lee's approval
to mass four brigades for a turning movement against the
Union's left flank. The Confederates, advancing along the bed of
an unfinished railroad that ran parallel to the Plank Road,
smashed into a position held by General David B. Birney, son of
antislavery leader James G. Birney. General Birney, a graduate
of Andover, had been trained in business and law, but he was
not much of a soldier. He owed his high military rank to

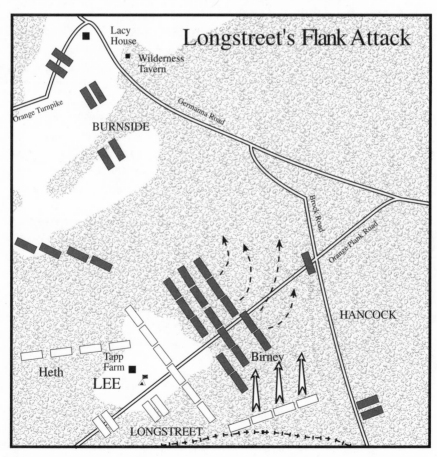

political influence. Longstreet's brigades rolled up Birney's line, in the words of General Hancock, "like a wet blanket."

No Federal demonstrated more courage in the wilderness than General James S. Wadsworth, commander of the Fourth Division of the Fifth Corps, who tenaciously maintained his position north of the Plank Road. When the colonel of a Massachusetts regiment argued that a counterattack would entail heavy casualties, Wadsworth announced that he would show the reluctant colonel how to attack, and galloped off to action. A member of the 17th Maine saw the general ride by: "he

General David B. Birney Born Alabama 1825; son of abolitionist James G. Birney; received his education at Andover; entered business; practiced law and engaged in business in Philadelphia during the 1850s; read on military subjects; became a

member of the historic 1st Troop of Philadelphia City Cavalry, and in 1860 was appointed lieutenant colonel of a regiment of Pennsylvania militia. In 1861 became colonel of the 23rd Pennsylvania Infantry; in 1862 appointed brigadier general of volunteers commanding a brigade in General Philip Kearny's Division; participated in the Peninsular Campaign, but was charged at Fair Oaks with having "halted his command a mile from the enemy"; a court martial acquitted him. Engaged in the Second Bull Run Campaign, taking temporary command of the division after Kearny's death at Chantilly; participated in the Battle of Fredericksburg; in 1863 he was promoted to major general of volunteers after the Battle of Chancellorsville; hit twice by enemy bullets but only slightly wounded at Gettysburg, where he commanded the Third Corps after General Daniel Sickles was wounded; in 1864 he took part in Grant's first campaign against Richmond, but after being given command of the Tenth Corps, Birney became seriously ill with malaria and died on October 11, 1864. His last words in delirium were, "Boys! Keep your eyes on that flag!" Friends characterized him as honest, gallant, and a self-sacrificing patriot.

was waving his sword over his head, his silvery hair shining like a meteor's glory. Without halting, without asking who we were, or informing us of himself, yet with the fury of battle in his eyes, he half turned and shouted: 'Forward! Forward!' and rode out beyond the woods into the open field still brandishing his sword and shouting 'forward!' It fairly took away our breaths."

Wadsworth's horse bolted and raced towards enemy lines. Confederates shot Wadsworth in the head, and he died two days later in a Confederate field hospital.

Longstreet, determined to extend his flanking movement east of the Brock Road, hoped to turn the enemy's extreme left and roll up the whole Federal army. As he rode forward, one of his brigade commanders, General Micah Jenkins, told his commander: "I am happy; I have felt despair for the cause for

General James S. Wadsworth Born New York 1807; spent two years at Harvard without graduating; studied law to prepare him to manage a large landed estate; never practiced law; in 1834 married Mary Craig Wharton; active in politics, but with no ambition for office; at first a Democrat; later his strong antislavery sentiments made him a Free-Soiler and then a Republican; delegate to the "peace conference" in Washington in 1861. Refused high military rank; served as an aide to General Irwin McDowell; commissioned brigadier general of volunteers after First Bull Run, but assigned to defense of Washington, D.C.; in 1862 accepted the Republican nomination for governor of New York, but was defeated; in 1863 played a small part in the Battle of Chancellorsville; fought effectively as commander of the First Division, First Corps, at Gettysburg; commanded the Fourth Division, Fifth Corps, in the Wilderness. After his death he was brevetted major general of volunteers for gallant  conduct at Gettysburg and the Wilderness. His friend John Lothrop Motley called Wadsworth "the truest and the most thoroughly loyal American I ever knew."

some months, but am relieved, and feel assured that we will put the enemy back across the Rapidan before night." Near the Brock Road Longstreet and his entourage heard firing. He had turned his horse and started toward the sound when a fierce volley from his own troops hit him and several of the officers accompanying him. Just one year before, Stonewall Jackson had fallen a victim of his own troops in the Wilderness during the Battle of Chancellorsville. When his soldiers saw Longstreet being carried from the field with his hat over his face, they shouted that he was dead. He later recalled uncovering his face with his left hand and that the resulting "burst of voices and the flying of hats in the air eased my pains somewhat." Though seriously wounded in the throat and right shoulder, Longstreet would live to fight again, but the wounds of Jenkins and two other officers were mortal. Jenkins, half-conscious, dying with a bullet in his brain, cheered "his men and implored them to sweep the enemy into the river till he was too weak to talk."

The wounding of Longstreet deprived the Confederate assault of momentum, but later in the afternoon Lee ordered another advance. "Before we formed in line," remembered a Federal soldier, "the Rebels were onto us in a furious charge." Lee had massed all his available forces in one supreme effort to overwhelm Hancock and get possession of the junction of the Plank and Brock roads.

It was a desperate encounter. Yelling like devils, the Confederates dashed against the Federal position. "Panic and confusion reigned and came near [to] resulting in a rout of the Union forces," admitted a Federal. The Union lines held, but at 5:30 P.M. Hancock informed Meade, "I do not think it advisable to attack [again] this evening."

By the time Hancock expressed his desire to end the day's combat, Lee was so fearful the Federals would counterattack that he had requested assistance from Ewell. "Cannot something be done," asked Lee, "to relieve the pressure upon

our right?" For the Army of Northern Virginia's commander—
shaken by the narrow escape of the morning, the wounding of
Longstreet, and the repulse of his last attack on the Federal left—
it had been "one of the most anxious days of his military career."

Ewell's front, by comparison, had been comparatively quiet

General Micah Jenkins Born South Carolina 1835; graduated in 1854 at the head
of his class from the Citadel; in 1855 cofounded King's Mountain Military School;
in 1856 married Caroline Jameson, whose father presided at the South Carolina
secession convention in 1860. Jenkins became colonel of the 5th South Carolina
Infantry in 1861; participated in the First Battle of Manassas; in 1862 he fought on
the Peninsula, at Seven Pines, and during the Seven Days' Battle, where he
frequently led General Richard H. Anderson's
Brigade and received praise for his gallantry from
Generals Joseph E. Johnston, James Longstreet,
and Daniel H. Hill; promoted to brigadier general in
July, Jenkins was severely wounded during the
Second Manassas Campaign at Chinn Ridge; he
and his brigade, part of General George E. Pickett's
Division, Longstreet's Corps, were at
Fredericksburg, but saw no combat; in 1863, after
accompanying Longstreet to Virginia south side
and participating in the Suffolk siege, Jenkins and
his men remained in Virginia and were not with
Pickett at Gettysburg. As senior officer, Jenkins
assumed command of Hood's Division, after Hood
was wounded at Chickamauga; following an

unsuccessful night attack at Wauhatchie, near Chattanooga, Jenkins and his
principal subordinate, General Evander M. Law, each blamed the other for the
defeat; feuding between Jenkins and Law continued during the Knoxville
Campaign; in 1864 Jenkins, replaced as division commander by General Charles
Field, returned with his brigade to the Army of Northern Virginia; he was killed in
the Wilderness on May 6, 1864. General D. H. Hill said that at Seven Pines
Jenkins's Brigade "rendered more service than any two engaged." General Arnold
Elzey considered Jenkins "one of the most gallant & meritorious officers in the
service." And General Lee once told the brave and handsome Jenkins: "I hope yet
to see you one of my lieutenant generals."

all day. Its only threat had been a feeble attempt by General Burnside's Ninth Corps to drive a wedge between Ewell's Corps and the rest of Lee's army, but the timely arrival of General Stephen Dodson Ramseur's Brigade of North Carolinians halted Burnside's advance. Ramseur attacked, "turned the enemy's line," and drove it "back fully half a mile." During their advance the Confederates captured prisoners and "copies of the Bible in the Ojibwa language dropped by members of a unit of Indian sharpshooters," who fought "bravely in the woods," but when "driven into the open, ran like deer." Ramseur, his biographer observed, "accomplished much at little cost." His movement

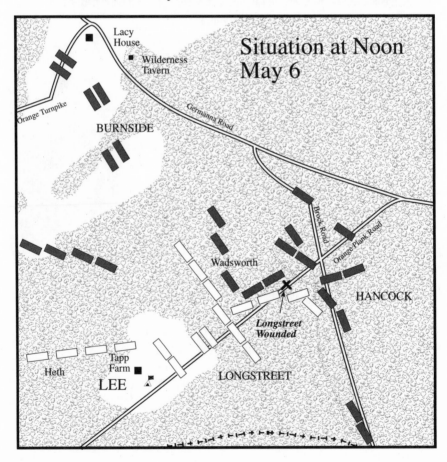

kept Ewell's right in contact with Hill's left and prevented
Burnside from interposing between them. At some time on the
afternoon of May 6 Lee met with Ewell and they decided to
attack the Federal right flank. When and where they met and
whether General John B. Gordon was present is uncertain, but
they adopted Gordon's attack plan—the one he had been
advocating all day. He had told Ewell and any superior officer
who would listen that the Federal army's extreme right flank,
which Gordon had examined that morning, was exposed.
"There was no line guarding this flank," he insisted. "As far as
my eye could reach, the Union soldiers were seated on the

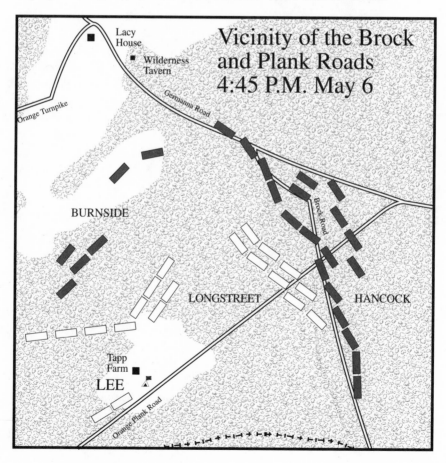

Vicinity of the Brock
and Plank Roads
4:45 P.M. May 6

General Ambrose E. Burnside Born Indiana 1824; apprenticed to a tailor and worked in a shop until friends of his father secured him an appointment to the U.S. Military Academy, where he graduated eighteenth in the class of 1847; appointed 2d lieutenant in 3rd Artillery in 1847, but saw little service in Mexico; promoted to 1st lieutenant in 1851; married Mary Richmond Bishop of Rhode Island in 1852 and resigned from army a year later to manufacture a breech-loading rifle he invented; company went bankrupt in 1857; major general in the Rhode Island militia and treasurer of the Illinois Central Railroad before the Civil War. In 1861 organized and became colonel of 1st Rhode Island Infantry, which was among the earliest regiments to reach Washington; became friend of President Lincoln and received promotion to brigadier general of volunteers August 1861 after

commanding a brigade at the Battle of Bull Run; in 1862 commanded a successful operation along the North Carolina Coast; commissioned a major general of volunteers and received awards and thanks from various states; twice offered but declined command of Army of the Potomac in 1862; at Antietam he wasted too much time crossing Antietam Creek and attacking the Confederate right. Finally accepted command of the Army of the Potomac, although he considered himself incompetent and proved himself correct by crossing the Rappahannock River in December 1862 and making a disastrous attack on the awaiting Confederate army at Fredericksburg; "I ought to retire to private life," Burnside informed President Lincoln, who after relieving him of command in the East assigned him to command the Department of the Ohio; at Lincoln's urging, he advanced into East Tennessee and in November 1863 repulsed an assault on Knoxville by Confederates under James Longstreet. Burnside and his Ninth Corps returned to the East in 1864 to serve under Grant from the Wilderness to Petersburg; blamed by General George Meade for the Union failure at the Crater, Burnside shortly thereafter went on leave and never returned to duty; in 1865 he resigned his commission. After the war he became president of various railroad and other companies; elected governor of Rhode Island in 1866 and reelected in 1867 and 1868; elected to U.S. Senate from Rhode Island in 1874, where he served until his death at Bristol, R.I., in 1881.

margin of the rifle pits, taking their breakfast. Small fires were burning over which they were boiling their coffee, while their guns leaned against the works in their immediate front." Gordon, certain that an attack would turn the Federal's right, possibly roll up, and maybe even destroy Grant's army, now had the right supporters. With Lee's approval, Ewell and his subordinate commanders quickly made preparations for the

General Stephen Dodson Ramseur Born North Carolina 1837; spent two years at Davidson College before entering the U.S. Military Academy from which he graduated fourteenth in the class of 1860; brevetted 2d lieutenant 3rd Artillery 1860; promoted to 2d lieutenant 4th Artillery 1861; resigned from U.S. Army before his state joined the Confederacy; appointed 1st lieutenant in Confederate artillery, he quickly moved up in rank to colonel of the 49th North Carolina Infantry in 1862; fought in the Seven Days' Battle as part of Ransom's Brigade where Ramseur suffered a critical wound to his right arm at Malvern Hill; promoted to brigadier general in November and in January 1863 given a brigade previously commanded by George B. Anderson; wounded again in May during the Battle of Chancellorsville; he fought at Gettysburg and Mine Run and married his cousin Ellen Richmond; in 1864 he turned back a Federal assault and filled a gap between Ewell's

and Hill's corps in the Wilderness; at Spotsylvania he helped restore the broken Confederate line and received a third wound and Lee's praise for his "unsurpassed gallantry"; promoted to major general and given a division in June, he fought at Bethesda Church and at Cold Harbor before accompanying Early's Corps to the Shenandoah Valley; fought at Winchester and Fisher's Hill. At Cedar Creek he received a mortal wound while wearing a full uniform with a flower in his lapel in honor of his new daughter. He died October 20, 1864. An officer noted that Ramseur "reveled in the fierce joys of the strife, his whole being seemed to kindle and burn and glow amid the excitements of danger." He was one of Lee's most aggressive and promising generals.

General John B. Gordon Born Georgia 1832; attended University of Georgia, but did not graduate; studied law; in 1856 entered his father's coal mining business; quickly became wealthy and entered politics; a Southern Rights Democrat, who favored secession. In 1861 he raised a company that joined the 6th Alabama Infantry, which elected him major; served but saw no action at First Manassas; promoted to colonel of the 6th Alabama and in 1862 transferred to General Robert E. Rodes's Brigade; during the Peninsula Campaign, after Rodes was wounded, Gordon commanded the brigade at Gaines' Mill and Malvern Hill; participated in the battles at South Mountain and Antietam, where five bullets struck him; his wife, who had left their two sons with her mother-in-law in Georgia, nursed him back to health. Promoted to brigadier general, he commanded a brigade in Jubal A. Early's

Division. "Not to promote him," said E. P. Alexander, "would have been a scandal." In 1863 Gordon won the respect of his men at Chancellorsville and Gettysburg; in 1864 in the Wilderness he delivered a crushing attack on the Union right. At Spotsylvania, commanding a division, his counterattack saved Lee's army; promoted to major general in May, he served under Early in the Shenandoah Valley Campaign, forcing General David O. Hunter from the valley and defeating General Lew Wallace at Monocacy; after failing to take Washington, D.C., Gordon and Early's Corps lost battles in September at Winchester and Fisher's Hill; a month later at Cedar Creek, Gordon executed a magnificent flanking movement, but his inability to control his hungry troops, who pillaged abandoned Yankee camps, outraged Early; their relationship deteriorated and hostility continued into the postwar years. In December Gordon rejoined Lee's forces defending Petersburg; in 1865 he directed an attack on Fort Stedman and then commanded the Second Corps on the retreat to Appomattox. After the war he served two and a half terms in the U.S. Senate (1873–80 and 1891–97) and one term as governor of Georgia (1886–90); engaged in various business interests; served as commander in chief of the United Confederate Veterans; published *Reminiscences of the Civil War* in 1903; he died in 1904. Six feet tall, thin, but with perfect posture, Gordon inspired confidence; officers called him "a picture for the sculptor" and "the very personification of a hero." But an admiring soldier offered the best description: "He's most the prettiest thing you ever did see on a field of fight. It'ud put fight into a whipped chicken just to look at him!"

attack. "They did all in their power," Gordon admitted years later, "to help forward the movement when once began."

The Federals were as unprepared as Gordon had promised. One of his Georgians recalled attacking the Yankees: "We found them all resting, cooking and eating; with their guns stacked, their blankets spread down and some of their little tents stretched. We came up in thick woods and were in about 100 yards of them before their guards saw us. We fired one volley at them, raised a yell and charged them." A major in the 122nd New York wrote in his diary: "Our regiment and the entire brigade were driven back in great confusion and with heavy loss; many of our regiment being killed and wounded and others falling and being taken prisoner."

Taken completely by surprise, regiment after regiment of Federals retreated. Gordon's delighted soldiers called the attack the "finest frolic" of the war. "My company struck the Federal breastworks squarely on the end," explained one Confederate. "I advanced up in rear of their works and at each step their confused mass became more dense."

Daniel M. Holt, surgeon of the 121st New York Volunteers, admitted that the Rebels forced his comrades into "a promiscuous skedaddle from...front to rear. My horse...had run off, as I ran after the horse I never made better time, nor ever came nearer to being gobbled up. After a flight of three miles we rally and form in line of battle. This has been a hard day and night for me—out all night—not a moment of sleep—dressing wounds and sending back disabled of all sorts. I gain a new dress suit entire in this skedaddle, but finding the owner gave them up after a while. It was this wise. Pell mell all were rushing along, horses *with* riders, and horses minus riders. An officer more intent on getting to the rear than to attend to his men, came pushing past my pack horse, and left [behind]...carpet bag containing his Sunday suit, &c. It was queer—this transferring baggage but true. My kit was long and protruding and caught the handle [of the carpetbag]...enough to take it off the saddle of—Surgeon [Melvin H.] Mansen 5th Maine—a *greater* coward if possible, than I."

Darkness and Union trenches eventually halted the action. By then, Gordon's men had killed or captured more than 1,000 Federals, and their prisoners included two brigadier generals. Confederate casualties amounted to about fifty. "I must be permitted to express the opinion that had the movement been made at an earlier hour and properly supported," Gordon reported, "it would have resulted in a decided disaster to the whole right wing of General Grant's army."

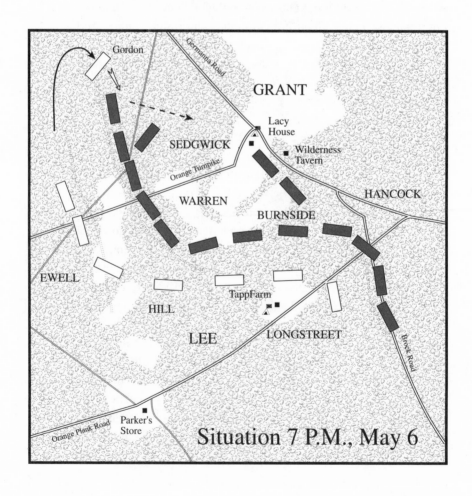

Situation 7 P.M., May 6

6

"THE COOLEST MAN
I EVER SAW"

Two days of fighting in the Wilderness had produced horrendous casualties. Grant lost about 18,000 men; Lee more than 11,000, some 7,000 from Hill's Corps alone. The dead and the dying were everywhere. With bodies sprawled in the bushes and against trees, the area around the Brock Road looked like an image of hell. Exhausted men staggered about, seeking refuge. The wounded who were too maimed to crawl screamed for help as the woods set afire by musketry burned toward them.

During all this gruesomeness, "the only sign of strain Grant showed," concluded his best biographer, "was that he smoked more than usual." Most of the time during the battle he "sat on a stump or lolled on the ground, incessantly smoking, frequently whittling, talking with Meade or with his own staff and apparently quite unexcited." People who saw Grant during the battle considered him to have been remarkably calm. A newspaperman called Grant "indescribably imperturbable," and a distinguished New Englander considered him "the coolest man I ever saw." Grant may have done little during the battle but "sit quietly about, whittle, [and] smoke," as General Marsena Patrick reported, but Grant probably was less calm than his outward manner revealed. During that ordeal of waiting, dressed in the full regalia of a lieutenant general, he managed to whittle holes in his new pair of yellow thread gloves.

In the past, after such a battle, Federal commanders usually retreated to regroup and to plan future movements, but

Casualties

not Grant. He was a different leader, engaged in a different type of warfare. Instead of retreating, he would try again to move around Lee's right flank. There would be no retreat by either army. On the morning of May 7, Grant directed Meade to prepare for a night march to Spotsylvania Court House.

The Wilderness had been neither a victory nor a defeat for either side. Lee had managed to turn both Federal flanks, but instead of retreating Grant decided to press on toward Richmond, giving the weakened Confederates no time to recover.

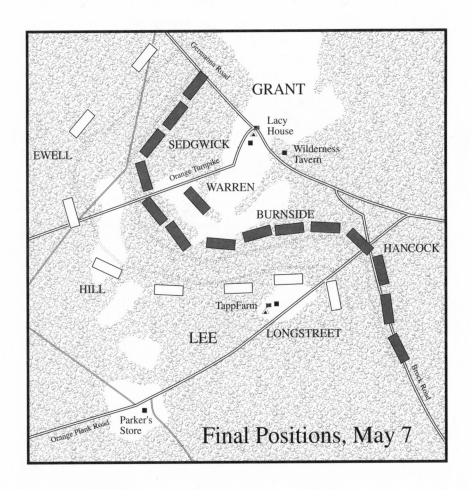

Final Positions, May 7

Lee won the race to Spotsylvania and had entrenched his army by the time Grant attacked on May 9. For more than a week, Federals struck at the Confederate defense line, but finally, unable to overwhelm Lee, Grant disengaged his army and once again moved around Lee's right toward Richmond. Of the approximately 90,000 Federals engaged, Grant lost 17,000; Lee probably lost 9,000 of his 50,000 Confederates. Although the Confederates had inflicted heavier losses on the Federals, Grant retained the initiative.

Surgeon Daniel Holt of the 121st New York Infantry summed up the fighting in the Wilderness and at Spotsylvania in a letter to his wife: "After eight days of the hardest fighting the world ever witnessed, I…am still alive and as yet unhurt. So fearful has been our loss, that it now seems we have no place here.… Heaven only knows how much longer this battle will last, but I hope not many days. No doubt we shall at last be victims. The rebels fight like very devils! We have to fairly club them out of their rifle pits. We have taken thousands of prisoners and killed an army; still they fight as hard as ever."

Each Federal movement cost Lee men he could ill afford to lose and brought Grant closer to Richmond. On May 23 the Federals encountered Lee's entrenched army along the North Anna River. After two days of skirmishing followed by a day of fighting, Grant broke off his attack and marched southward to Mechanicsville. There he found Lee's main line too strong and moved south a fourth time to discover the dauntless Lee dug in again at Cold Harbor. After inadequate reconnaissance, Grant sent three Union corps against Lee's strong fieldworks. The main attack failed, although smaller actions continued for several days. Grant suffered a bloody defeat at Cold Harbor, where he lost 7,000 men; Lee lost only 1,500.

On June 12 Grant began moving his army south of the James River where he linked up with General Butler's army on the outskirts of Petersburg, just south of Richmond. This maneuver fooled Lee for a time, but the uncoordinated Federal assaults failed to drive the outnumbered Confederates from Petersburg, and by June 22 Lee arrived with the main part of his army. Tedious trench warfare followed, foreshadowing the terrible carnage on the Western Front in World War I. For the remainder of the year Grant extended his entrenchments southward and westward trying to cut Lee's supply lines. To meet this threat, Lee stretched his defense ever thinner. By winter there was only one railroad open to Petersburg.

As Grant moved toward Richmond, Sherman moved south from Chattanooga toward Atlanta. Using his army of 100,000 men in flanking movements, he pushed Joseph E. Johnston's Confederates back across northern Georgia. Checked when he attacked strong fieldworks at Kennesaw Mountain, Sherman quickly returned to his more successful and less costly flanking movements. When the Confederates eventually fell back to the outskirts of Atlanta, President Davis replaced Johnston with General John Bell Hood. Sherman, guessing correctly that Hood would attack, prepared his army. In nine days Sherman defeated Hood three times, and then cut Atlanta's supply lines, forcing Hood to get out or starve. Hood abandoned the town, which Sherman occupied on September 2. After abandoning Atlanta, Hood moved north and west into Tennessee. He hoped to achieve victories that would offset not only his loss of Atlanta but Union Admiral David Farragut's victory in Mobile Bay, which closed the Confederacy's last big seaport on the Gulf. Hood had fantastic plans: defeat the Federals, recruit new soldiers in Tennessee, and then move eastward to reinforce Lee.

Sherman's counterplans were more realistic. Leaving behind General George H. Thomas and enough troops to contain Hood, Sherman moved from Atlanta southeastward across Georgia with 62,000 men toward Savannah on his "March to the Sea." Thomas rushed to fortify Nashville and sent General John Schofield to watch Hood's movements. Schofield, after escaping from a fight at Columbia and a trap at Spring Hill, withdrew northward to Franklin, Tennessee, where his 28,000 troops hastily dug fieldworks.

Hood followed and sent his 23,000 Confederates in a grand assault across a half mile of open ground against the Federal entrenchments. It proved a disaster for the Confederates, who lost more than 6,000 men, including six generals killed, five wounded, and one captured. The Federals suffered only a few more than 1,000 casualties.

After Franklin, Hood continued on to Nashville and placed his demoralized army on hills outside the town. In two days of fighting in mid-December, Thomas's 50,000 troops crushed Hood's weak line. After losing twice as many men as the Federals, Hood retreated. Nashville was his last battle, and as the wreckage of the Confederate army limped southward, a few wits sang: "The Gallant Hood of Texas Played Hell in Tennessee."

While Hood was destroying his army, Sherman marched through Georgia and the Carolinas, carrying out a policy of total war. After burning Atlanta, he moved toward Savannah methodically destroying anything that might be useful to the Confederacy. Promising Georgia's governor that he would "devastate the State in its whole length and breadth," Sherman informed Grant: "Until we can repopulate Georgia, it is useless for us to occupy it; but [its] utter destruction will cripple their military resources. I can make Georgia howl." Indeed he did. Sherman's 60,000 men, marching along four parallel roads, laid waste a strip of country sixty miles wide and three hundred miles long. Small Confederate units sniped at Sherman's troops, but no major army opposed the Federals. On December 22, Sherman captured Savannah and presented it to Lincoln as a Christmas gift. Estimating that his troops had inflicted $100,000,000 worth of damage on Georgia, Sherman admitted that 80 percent of this was "simple waste and destruction."

The Federals remained in Savannah about a month and then, with his army stronger than ever, Sherman moved through South Carolina and into North Carolina. Joseph E. Johnston, who had scraped together about 15,000 Confederates, attacked one wing of Sherman's army at Bentonville, North Carolina, on March 19–20, 1865. Johnston's troops held their own until the remainder of Sherman's army arrived and forced them to withdraw. Sherman seized the railroad at Goldsboro and bivouacked to await word from Grant.

Lee's army still held the Petersburg trenches, but the men had suffered through the long winter months. Food supplies shrank and bitterly cold weather sickened hungry men dressed in rags and without overcoats or tents. Disease plagued the Confederates; their numbers dwindled to 28,000 men as Grant continued a slow extension of the Union lines. Lee had no choice but to lengthen his own lines. On March 25, 1865, he lost 5,000 soldiers in a desperate attempt to break Grant's hold at the north end of the siege line. Having secured his right, Grant sent Sheridan on April 1 to the far left to gain control of Lee's only remaining supply line—the South Side Railroad. The Confederates resisted, but Sheridan's numbers overwhelmed them. Grant then attacked all along the Petersburg line, and Lee's thin defenses collapsed. Lee managed to hold on long enough for the Confederate government to abandon Richmond, but he failed in his effort to join Johnston's army. On April 9, after losing a third of his men in a bloody fight at Sayler's Creek, Lee surrendered his encircled army of 13,000 men to Grant at Appomattox.

Note: The Tables of Organization presented in Appendices A and B are taken from *War of the Rebellion: Official Records of the Union and Confederate Armies*, Series I, Volume 36, Part 1, Pages 106–116 and 1021-1027, Republished by The National Historical Society, 1972.

APPENDIX A

ORGANIZATION OF FEDERAL FORCES

COMMANDER IN CHIEF
LIEUT. GEN. ULYSSES S. GRANT

ARMY OF THE POTOMAC
MAJ. GEN. GEORGE G. MEADE

PROVOST GUARD
BRIG. GEN. MARSENA R. PATRICK

1st Massachusetts Cavalry, Companies C and D, Capt. Edward A. Flint
80th New York Infantry (20th Militia), Col. Theodore B. Gates
3d Pennsylvania Cavalry, Maj. James W. Walsh
68th Pennsylvania Infantry, Lieut. Col. Robert E. Winslow
114th Pennsylvania Infantry, Col. Charles H. T. Collis

VOLUNTEER ENGINEER BRIGADE
BRIG. GEN. HENRY W. BENHAM

15th New York Engineers, Maj. William A. Ketchum
50th New York Engineers, (eleven companies of this regiment and its
          commander, Lieut. Col. Ira Spaulding, were at the
          Engineer Depot, Washington, D.C.)

BATTALION U. S. ENGINEERS
CAPT. GEORGE H. MENDELL

GUARDS AND ORDERLIES
Independent Company Oneida (New York) Cavalry, Capt. Daniel P. Mann

SECOND ARMY CORPS
MAJ. GEN. WINFIELD S. HANCOCK

ESCORT

1st Vermont Cavalry, Company M, Capt. John H. Hazelton

FIRST DIVISION

BRIG. GEN. FRANCIS C. BARLOW

First Brigade

COL. NELSON A. MILES

26th Michigan, Maj. Lemuel Saviers
61st New York, Lieut. Col. K. Oscar Broady
81st Pennsylvania, Col. H. Boyd McKeen
140th Pennsylvania, Col. John Fraser
183d Pennsylvania, Col. George P. McLean

Second Brigade

COL. THOMAS A. SMYTH

28th Massachusetts, Lieut. Col. George W. Cartwright
63d New York, Maj. Thomas Touhy
69th New York, Capt. Richard Moroney
88th New York, Capt. Denis F. Burke
116th Pennsylvania, Lieut. Col. Richard C. Dale

Third Brigade

COL. PAUL FRANK

39th New York, Col. Augustus Funk
52d New York (including part of 7th New York), Maj. Henry M. Karples
57th New York, Lieut. Col. Alford B. Chapman
111th New York, Capt. Aaron P. Seeley
125th New York, Lieut. Col. Aaron B. Myer
126th New York, Capt. Winfield Scott

Fourth Brigade

COL. JOHN R. BROOKE

2d Delaware, Col. William P. Baily
64th New York, Maj. Leman W. Bradley
66th New York, Lieut. Col. John S. Hammell
53d Pennsylvania, Lieut. Col. Richard McMichael
145th Pennsylvania, Col. Hiram L. Brown
148th Pennsylvania, Col. James A. Beaver

SECOND DIVISION
BRIG. GEN. JOHN GIBBON

Provost Guard
2d Company Minnesota Sharpshooters, Capt. Mahlon Black

First Brigade
BRIG. GEN. ALEXANDER S. WEBB
19th Maine, Col. Selden Connor
1st Company Andrew (Massachusetts) Sharpshooters,
    Lieut. Samuel G. Gilbreth
15th Massachusetts, Maj. I. Harris Hooper
19th Massachusetts, Maj. Edmund Rice
20th Massachusetts, Maj. Henry L. Abbott
7th Michigan, Maj. Sylvanus W. Curtis
42d New York, Maj. Patrick J. Downing
59th New York, Capt. William McFadden
82d New York (2d Militia) Col. Henry W. Hudson

Second Brigade
BRIG. GEN. JOSHUA T. OWEN
152d New York, Lieut. Col. George W. Thompson
69th Pennsylvania, Maj. William Davis
71st Pennsylvania, Lieut. Col. Charles Kochersperger
72d Pennsylvania, Col. De Witt C. Baxter
106th Pennsylvania, Capt. Robert H. Ford

Third Brigade
COL. SAMUEL S. CARROLL
14th Connecticut, Col. Theodore G. Ellis
1st Delaware, Lieut. Col. Daniel Woodall
14th Indiana, Col. John Coons
12th New Jersey, Lieut. Col. Thomas H. Davis
10th New York Battalion, Capt. George M. Dewey
108th New York, Col. Charles J. Powers
4th Ohio, Lieut. Col. Leonard W. Carpenter
8th Ohio, Lieut. Col. Franklin Sawyer
7th West Virginia, Lieut. Col. Jonathan H. Lockwood

THIRD DIVISION
MAJ. GEN. DAVID B. BIRNEY

First Brigade
BRIG. GEN. J. H. HOBART WARD
20th Indiana, Col. William C. L. Taylor
3d Maine, Col. Moses B. Lakeman
40th New York,Col. Thomas W. Egan
86th New York, Lieut. Col. Jacob H. Lansing
124th New York, Col. Francis M. Cummins
99th Pennsylvania, Lieut. Col. Edwin R. Biles
110th Pennsylvania, Lieut. Col. Isaac Rogers
141st Pennsylvania, Lieut. Col. Guy H. Watkins
2d U. S. Sharpshooters, Lieut Col. Homer R. Stoughton

Second Brigade
BRIG. GEN. ALEXANDER HAYS
4th Maine, Col. Elijah Walker
17th Maine, Col. George W. West
3d Michigan, Col. Byron R. Pierce
5th Michigan, Lieut. Col. John Pulford
93d New York, Maj. Samuel McConihe
57th Pennsylvania, Col. Peter Sides
63d Pennsylvania, Lieut. Col. John A. Danks
105th Pennsylvania, Col. Calvin A. Craig
1st U.S. Sharpshooters, Maj. Charles P. Mattocks

FOURTH DIVISION
BRIG. GEN. GERSHOM MOTT

First Brigade
COL. ROBERT MCALLISTER
1st Massachusetts, Col. Napoleon B. McLaughlen
16th Massachusetts, Lieut. Col. Waldo Merriam
5th New Jersey, Col. William J. Sewell
6th New Jersey, Lieut. Col. Stephen R. Gilkyson
7th New Jersey, Maj. Frederick Cooper
8th New Jersey, Col. John Ramsey
11th New Jersey, Lieut. Col. John Schoonover
26th Pennsylvania, Maj. Samuel G. Moffett
115th Pennsylvania, Maj. William A. Reilly

Second Brigade
COL. WILLIAM R. BREWSTER
11th Massachusetts, Col. William Blaisdell
70th New York, Capt. William H. Hugo
71st New York, Lieut. Col. Thomas Rafferty
72d New York, Lieut. Col. John Leonard
73d New York, Lieut. Col. Michael W. Burns
74th New York, Col. Thomas Holt
120th New York, Capt. Abram L. Lockwood
84th Pennsylvania, Lieut. Col. Milton Opp

ARTILLERY BRIGADE
COL. JOHN C. TIDBALL
Maine Light, 6th Battery (F), Capt. Edwin B. Dow
Massachusetts Light, 10th Battery, Capt. J. Henry Sleeper
New Hampshire Light, 1st Battery, Capt. Frederick M. Edgell
1st New York Light, Battery G, Capt. Nelson Ames
4th New York Heavy, 3d Battalion, Lieut. Col. Thomas Allcock
1st Pennsylvania Light, Battery F, Capt. R. Bruce Ricketts
1st Rhode Island Light, Battery A, Capt. William A. Arnold
1st Rhode Island Light, Battery B, Capt. T. Frederick Brown
4th United States, Battery K, Lieut. John W. Roder
5th United States, Batteries C and I, Lieut. James Gilliss

FIFTH ARMY CORPS
MAJ. GEN. GOUVERNEUR K. WARREN

PROVOST GUARD
12TH NEW YORK BATTALION, MAJ. HENRY W. RIDER

FIRST DIVISION
BRIG. GEN. CHARLES GRIFFIN

First Brigade
B. G. ROMEYN B. AYRES
140th New York, Col. George Ryan
146th New York, Col. David T. Jenkins
91st Pennsylvania, Lieut. Col. Joseph H. Sinex
155th Pennsylvania, Lieut. Col. Alfred L. Pearson

2d United States, Companies B, C, F, H, I, and K,
   Capt. James W. Long
11th United States, Companies B, C, D, E, F, and G, First Battalion,
   Capt. Francis M. Cooley
12th United States, Companies A, B, C, D, and G, 1st Battalion,
   Maj. Luther B. Bruen
12th United States, Companies A, C, D, F, and H, 2d Battalion,
   Maj. Luther B. Bruen
14th United States, 1st Battalion, Capt. Edward McK. Hudson
17th United States, Companies A, C, D, G, and H, 1st Battalion,
   Capt. James F. Grimes
17th United States, Companies A, B, and C, 2d Battalion,
   Capt. James F. Grimes

Second Brigade
COL. JACOB B. SWEITZER

9th Massachusetts, Col. Patrick R. Guiney
22d Massachusetts (2d Company Massachusetts Sharpshooters
   attached), Col. William S. Tilton
32nd Massachusetts, Col. George L. Prescott
4th Michigan, Lieut. Col. George W. Lumbard
62d Pennsylvania, Lieut. Col. James C. Hull

Third Brigade
BRIG. GEN. JOSEPH J. BARTLETT

20th Maine, Maj. Ellis Spear
18th Massachusetts, Col. Joseph Hayes
1st Michigan, Lieut. Col. William A. Throop
16th Michigan, Maj. Robert T. Elliott
44th New York, Lieut. Col. Freeman Conner
83d Pennsylvania, Col. Orpheus S. Woodward
118th Pennsylvania, Col. James Gwyn

SECOND DIVISION
BRIG. GEN. JOHN C. ROBINSON

First Brigade
COL. SAMUEL H. LEONARD
16th Maine, Col. Charles W. Tilden
13th Massachusetts, Capt. Charles H. Hovey
39th Massachusetts, Col. Phineas S. Davis
104th New York, Col. Gilbert G. Prey

Second Brigade
BRIG. GEN. HENRY BAXTER
12th Massachusetts, Col. James L. Bates
83d New York (9th Militia), Col. Joseph A. Moesch
97th New York, Col. Charles Wheelock
11th Pennsylvania, Col. Richard Coulter
88th Pennsylvania, Capt. George B. Rhoads
90th Pennsylvania, Col. Peter Lyle

Third Brigade
COL. ANDREW W. DENISON
1st Maryland, Maj. Benjamin H. Schley
4th Maryland, Col. Richard N. Bowerman
7th Maryland, Col. Charles E. Phelps
8th Maryland, Lieut. Col. John G. Johannes

THIRD DIVISION
BRIG. GEN. SAMUEL W. CRAWFORD

First Brigade
COL. WILLIAM MCCANDLESS
1st Pennsylvania Reserves, Col. William C. Talley
2d Pennsylvania Reserves, Lieut. Col. Patrick McDonough
6th Pennsylvania Reserves, Col. Wellington H. Ent
7th Pennsylvania Reserves, Maj. LeGrand B. Speece
11th Pennsylvania Reserves, Col. Samuel M. Jackson
13th Pennsylvania Reserves (1st Rifles), Maj. William R. Hartshorne

Third Brigade
COL. JOSEPH W. FISHER

5th Pennsylvania Reserves, Lieut. Col. George Dare
8th Pennsylvania Reserves, Col. Silas M. Baily
10th Pennsylvania Reserves, Lieut. Col. Ira Ayer, Jr.
12th Pennsylvania Reserves, Lieut. Col. Richard Gustin

FOURTH DIVISION
BRIG. GEN. JAMES S. WADSWORTH

First Brigade
BRIG. GEN. LYSANDER CUTLER

7th Indiana, Col. Ira G. Grover
19th Indiana, Col. Samuel J. Williams
24th Michigan, Col. Henry A. Morrow
1st New York Battalion Sharpshooters, Capt. Volney J. Shipman
2d Wisconsin, Lieut. Col. John Mansfield
6th Wisconsin, Col. Edward S. Bragg
7th Wisconsin, Col. William W. Robinson

Second Brigade
BRIG. GEN. JAMES C. RICE

76th New York, Lieut. Col. John E. Cook
84th New York (14th Militia), Col. Edward B. Fowler
95th New York, Col. Edward Pye
147th New York, Col. Francis C. Miller
56th Pennsylvania, Col. J. William Hofmann

Third Brigade
COL. ROY STONE

121st Pennsylvania, Capt. Samuel T. Lloyd
142d Pennsylvania, Maj. Horatio N. Warren
143d Pennsylvania, Col. Edmund L. Dana
149th Pennsylvania, Lieut. Col. John Irvin
150th Pennsylvania, Capt. George W. Jones

ARTILLERY BRIGADE

COL. CHARLES S. WAINWRIGHT

Massachusetts Light, Battery C, Capt. Augustus P. Martin

Massachusetts Light, Battery E, Capt. Charles A. Phillips

1st New York Light, Battery D, Capt. George B. Winslow

1st New York Light, Batteries E and L, Lieut. George Breck

1st New York Light, Battery H, Capt. Charles E. Mink

4th New York Heavy, 2d Battalion, Maj. William Arthur

1st Pennsylvania Light, Battery B, Capt. James H. Cooper

4th United States, Battery B, Lieut. James Stewart

5th United States, Battery D, Lieut. Benjamin F. Rittenhouse

SIXTH ARMY CORPS

MAJ. GEN. JOHN SEDGWICK

ESCORT

8th Pennsylvania Cavalry, Company A, Capt. Charles E. Fellows.

FIRST DIVISION

BRIG. GEN. HORATIO G. WRIGHT

First Brigade

COL. HENRY W. BROWN

1st New Jersey, Lieut. Col. William Henry, Jr

2d New Jersey, Lieut. Col. Charles Wiebecke

3d New Jersey, Capt. Samuel T. Du Bois

4th New Jersey, Lieut. Col. Charles Ewing

10th New Jersey, Col. Henry O. Ryerson

15th New Jersey, Col. William H. Penrose

Second Brigade

COL. EMORY UPTON

5th Maine, Col. Clark S. Edwards

121st New York, Lieut. Col. Egbert Olcott

95th Pennsylvania, Lieut. Col. Edward Carroll

96th Pennsylvania, Lieut. Col. William H. Lessig

Third Brigade
BRIG. GEN. DAVID A. RUSSELL

6th Maine, Maj. George Fuller
49th Pennsylvania, Col. Thomas M. Hulings
119th Pennsylvania, Maj. Henry P. Truefitt, Jr.
5th Winsconsin, Lieut. Col. Theodore B. Catlin

Fourth Brigade
BRIG. GEN. ALEXANDER SHALER

65th New York, Col. Joseph E. Hamblin
67th New York, Col. Nelson Cross
122d New York, Lieut. Col. Augustus W. Dwight
82d Pennsylvania (detachment), —[1]

SECOND DIVISION
BRIG. GEN. GEORGE W. GETTY

First Brigade
BRIG. GEN. FRANK WHEATON

62d New York, Col. David J. Nevin
93d Pennsylvania, Lieut. Col. John S. Long
98th Pennsylvania, Col. John F. Ballier
102d Pennsylvania, Col. John W. Patterson
139th Pennsylvania, Lieut. Col. William H. Moody

Second Brigade
COL. LEWIS A. GRANT

2d Vermont, Col. Newton Stone
3d Vermont, Col. Thomas O. Seaver
4th Vermont, Col. George P. Foster
5th Vermont, Lieut. Col. John R. Lewis
6th Vermont, Col. Elisha L. Barney

Third Brigade
BRIG. GEN. THOMAS H. NEILL

7th Maine, Col. Edwin C. Mason
43d New York, Lieut. Col. John Wilson
49th New York, Col. Daniel D. Bidwell
77th New York, Maj. Nathan S. Babcock
61st Pennsylvania, Col. George F. Smith

[1] A dash after the name of a unit indicates that the commanding officer's name is not known.

Fourth Brigade
BRIG. GEN. HENRY L. EUSTIS
7th Massachusetts, Col. Thomas D. Johns
10th Massachusetts, Lieut. Col. Joseph B. Parsons
37th Massachusetts, Col. Oliver Edwards
2d Rhode Island, Lieut. Col. Samuel B. M. Read

THIRD DIVISION
BRIG. GEN. JAMES B. RICKETTS

First Brigade
BRIG. GEN. WILLIAM H. MORRIS
14th New Jersey, Lieut. Col. Caldwell K. Hall
106th New York, Lieut. Col. Charles Townsend
151st New York, Lieut. Col. Thomas M. Fay
87th Pennsylvania, Col. John W. Schall
10th Vermont, Lieut. Col. William W. Henry

Second Brigade
BRIG. GEN. TRUMAN SEYMOUR
6th Maryland, Col. John W. Horn
110th Ohio, Col. J. Warren Keifer
122d Ohio, Col. William H. Ball
126th Ohio, Col. Benjamin F. Smith
67th Pennsylvania (detachment), Capt. George W. Guss
138th Pennsylvania, Col. Matthew R. McClennan

ARTILLERY BRIGADE
COL. CHARLES H. TOMPKINS
Maine Light, 4th Battery (D), Lieut. Melville C. Kimball
Massachusetts Light, 1st Battery (A), Capt. William H. McCartney
New York Light, 1st Battery, Capt. Andrew Cowan
New York Light, 3rd Battery, Capt. William A. Harn
4th New York Heavy, 1st Battalion, Maj. Thomas D. Sears
1st Rhode Island Light, Battery C, Capt. Richard Waterman
1st Rhode Island Light, Battery E, Capt. William B. Rhodes
1st Rhode Island Light, Battery G, Capt. George W. Adams
5th United States, Battery M, Capt. James McKnight

NINTH ARMY CORPS [2]
MAJ. GEN. AMBROSE E. BURNSIDE

PROVOST GUARD
8TH U. S. INFANTRY, CAPT. MILTON COGSWELL

FIRST DIVISION
BRIG. GEN. THOMAS G. STEVENSON

First Brigade
COL. SUMNER CARRUTH

35th Massachusetts, Maj. Nathaniel Wales
56th Massachusetts, Col. Charles E. Griswold
57th Massachusetts, Col. William F. Bartlett
59th Massachusetts, Col. J. Parker Gould
4th United States, Capt. Charles H. Brightly
10th United States, Maj. Samuel B. Hayman

Second Brigade
COL. DANIEL LEASURE

3d Maryland, Col. Joseph M. Sudsburg
21st Massachusetts, Lieut. Col. George P. Hawkes
100th Pennsylvania, Lieut. Col. Matthew M. Dawson

Artillery
Maine Light, 2d Battery (B), Capt. Albert F. Thomas
Massachusetts Light, 14th Battery, Capt. Joseph W. B. Wright

SECOND DIVISION
BRIG. GEN. ROBERT B. POTTER

First Brigade
COL. ZENAS R. BLISS

36th Massachusetts, Maj. William F. Draper
58th Massachusetts, Lieut. Col. John C. Whiton
51st New York, Col. Charles W. LeGendre
45th Pennsylvania, Col. John I. Curtin
48th Pennsylvania, Lieut. Col. Henry Pleasants
7th Rhode Island, Capt. Theodore Winn

---

[2] This corps was under the direct orders of Lieut. General Ulysses S. Grant until May 24th, 1864, when it was assigned to the Army of the Potomac.

Second Brigade
Col. Simon G. Griffin
31st Maine, Lieut. Col. Thomas Hight
32d Maine, Maj. Arthur Deering
6th New Hampshire, Lieut. Col. Henry H. Pearson
9th New Hampshire, Lieut. Col. John W. Babbitt
11th New Hampshire, Col. Walter Harriman
17th Vermont, Lieut. Col. Charles Cummings

Artillery
Massachusetts Light, 11th Battery, Capt. Edward J. Jones
New York Light, 19th Battery, Capt. Edward W. Rogers

THIRD DIVISION
Brig. Gen. Orlando B. Willcox

First Brigade
Col. John F. Hartranft
2d Michigan, Col. William Humphrey
8th Michigan, Col. Frank Graves
17th Michigan, Col. Constant Luce
27th Michigan (1st and 2d Companies Michigan Sharpshooters
    attached), Maj. Samuel Moody
109th New York, Col. Benjamin F. Tracy
51st Pennsylvania, Lieut. Col. Edwin Schall

Second Brigade
Col. Benjamin C. Christ
1st Michigan Sharpshooters, Col. Charles V. De Land
20th Michigan, Lieut. Col. Byron M. Cutcheon
79th New York, Col. David Morrison
60th Ohio (9th and 10th Companies Ohio Sharpshooters attached),
    Lieut. Col. James N. McElroy
50th Pennsylvania, Lieut. Col. Edward Overton, Jr.

Artillery
Maine Light, 7th Battery (G), Capt. Adelbert B. Twitchell
New York Light, 34th Battery, Capt. Jacob Roemer

FOURTH DIVISION
Brig. Gen. Edward Ferrero

First Brigade
Col. Joshua K. Sigfried
27th U. S. Colored Troops, Lieut. Col. Charles J. Wright
30th U. S. Colored Troops, Col. Delavan Bates
39th U. S. Colored Troops, Col. Ozora P. Stearns
43rd U. S. Colored Troops, Lieut. Col. H. Seymour Hall

Second Brigade
Col. Henry G. Thomas
30th Connecticut (colored), detachment, Capt. Charles Robinson
19th U. S. Colored Troops, Lieut. Col. Joseph G. Perkins
23d U. S. Colored Troops, Lieut. Col. Cleaveland J. Campbell.

Artillery
Pennsylvania Light, Battery D, Capt. George W. Durell
Vermont Light, 3d Battery, Capt. Romeo H. Start

CAVALRY
3d New Jersey, Col. Andrew J. Morrison
22d New York, Col. Samuel J. Crooks
2d Ohio, Lieut. Col. George A. Purington
13th Pennsylvania, Maj. Michael Kerwin

RESERVE ARTILLERY
Capt. John Edwards, Jr.
New York Light, 27th Battery, Capt. John B. Eaton
1st Rhode Island Light, Battery D, Capt. William W. Buckley
1st Rhode Island Light, Battery H, Capt. Crawford Allen, Jr.
2d United States, Battery E, Lieut. James S. Dudley
3d United States, Battery G, Lieut. Edmund Pendleton
3d United States, Batteries L and M, Lieut. Erskine Gittings

PROVISIONAL BRIGADE
Col. Elisha G. Marshall
24th New York Cavalry (dismounted), Col. William C. Raulston
14th New York Heavy Artillery, Lieut. Col. Clarence H. Corning
2d Pennsylvania Provisional Heavy Artillery, Col. Thomas Wilhelm

CAVALRY CORPS
MAJ. GEN. PHILIP H. SHERIDAN

ESCORT
6th United States, Capt. Ira W. Claflin

FIRST DIVISION
BRIG. GEN. ALFRED T. A. TORBERT

First Brigade
BRIG. GEN. GEORGE A. CUSTER
1st Michigan, Lieut. Col. Peter Stagg
5th Michigan, Col. Russell A. Alger
6th Michigan, Maj. James H. Kidd
7th Michigan, Maj. Henry W. Granger

Second Brigade
COL. THOMAS C. DEVIN
4th New York (detached guarding trains), Lieut. Col. William R. Parnell
6th New York, Lieut. Col. William H. Crocker
9th New York, Col. William Sackett
17th Pennsylvania, Lieut. Col. James Q. Anderson

Reserve Brigade
BRIG. GEN. WESLEY MERRITT
19th New York (1st Dragoons), Col. Alfred Gibbs
6th Pennsylvania, Maj. James Starr
1st United States, Capt. Nelson B. Sweitzer
2d United States, Capt. Theophilus F. Rodenbough
5th United States (Companies B, F, and K, under Capt. Julius W. Mason, detached as escort to Gen. Grant), Capt. Abraham K. Arnold

SECOND DIVISION
BRIG. GEN. DAVID McM. GREGG

First Brigade
BRIG. GEN. HENRY E. DAVIES, JR.
1st Massachusetts, Maj. Lucius M. Sargent
1st New Jersey, Lieut. Col. John W. Kester
6th Ohio, Col. William Stedman
1st Pennsylvania, Col. John P. Taylor

Second Brigade
COL. J. IRVIN GREGG
1st Maine, Col. Charles H. Smith
10th New York, Maj. M. Henry Avery
2d Pennsylvania, Lieut. Col. Joseph P. Brinton
4th Pennsylvania, Lieut. Col. George H. Covode
8th Pennsylvania, Lieut. Col. Samuel Wilson
16th Pennsylvania, Lieut. Col. John K. Robison

THIRD DIVISION
BRIG. GEN. JAMES H. WILSON

Escort
8th Illinois (detachment), Lieut. William W. Long

First Brigade
COL. TIMOTHY M. BRYAN, JR.
COL. JOHN B. McINTOSH (ASSIGNED MAY 5)
1st Connecticut, Maj. Erastus Blakeslee
2d New York, Col. Otto Harhaus
5th New York, Lieut. Col. John Hammond
18th Pennsylvania, Lieut. Col. William P. Brinton

Second Brigade
COL. GEORGE H. CHAPMAN
3d Indiana, Maj. William Patton
8th New York, Lieut. Col. William H. Benjamin
1st Vermont, Lieut. Col. Addison W. Preston

ARTILLERY
BRIG. GEN. HENRY J. HUNT

ARTILLERY RESERVE
COL. HENRY S. BURTON

First Brigade
COL. J. HOWARD KITCHING
6th New York Heavy, Lieut. Col. Edmund R. Travis
15th New York Heavy, Col. Louis Schirmer

Second Brigade
MAJ. JOHN A. TOMPKINS
Maine Light, 5th Battery (E), Capt. Greenleaf T. Stevens
1st New Jersey Light, Battery A, Capt. William Hexamer
1st New Jersey Light, Battery B, Capt. A. Judson Clark
New York Light, 5th Battery, Capt. Elijah D. Taft
New York Light, 12th Battery, Capt. George F. McKnight
1st New York Light, Battery B, Capt. Albert S. Sheldon

Third Brigade
MAJ. ROBERT H. FITZHUGH
Massachusetts Light, 9th Battery, Capt. John Bigelow
New York Light, 15th Battery, Capt. Patrick Hart
1st New York Light, Battery C, Lieut. William H. Phillips
New York Light, 11th Battery, Capt. John E. Burton
1st Ohio Light, Battery H, Lieut. William A. Ewing
5th United States, Battery E, Lieut. John R. Brinckle

HORSE ARTILLERY
First Brigade (detached with Cavalry Corps)
CAPT. JAMES M. ROBERTSON
New York Light, 6th Battery, Capt. Joseph W. Martin
2d United States, Batteries B and L, Lieut. Edward Heaton
2d United States, Battery D, Lieut. Edward B. Williston
2d United States, Battery M, Lieut. Alexander C. M. Pennington, Jr.
4th United States, Battery A, Lieut. Rufus King, Jr.
4th United States, Batteries C and E, Lieut. Charles L. Fitzhugh

Second Brigade
CAPT. DUNBAR R. RANSOM
1st United States, Batteries E and G, Lieut. Frank S. French
1st United States, Batteries H and I, Capt. Alanson M. Randol
1st United States, Battery K, Lieut. John Egan
2d United States, Battery A, Lieut. Robert Clarke
2d United States, Battery G, Lieut. William N. Dennison
3d United States, Batteries C, F, and K, Lieut. James R. Kelly

APPENDIX B

ORGANIZATION OF CONFEDERATE FORCES
ARMY OF NORTHERN VIRGINIA
GEN. ROBERT E. LEE

FIRST ARMY CORPS
LT. GEN. JAMES LONGSTREET

KERSHAW'S DIVISION
BRIG. GEN. JOSEPH B. KERSHAW

Kershaw's Brigade
COL. JOHN W. HENAGAN
2d South Carolina, Lieut. Col. Franklin Gaillard
3d South Carolina, Col. James D. Nance
7th South Carolina, Capt. James Mitchell
8th South Carolina, Lieut. Col. Eli T. Stackhouse
15th South Carolina, Col. John B. Davis
3d South Carolina Battalion, Capt. B. M. Whitener

Wofford's Brigade
BRIG. GEN. WILLIAM T. WOFFORD
16th Georgia, —[1]
18th Georgia, —
24th Georgia, —
Cobb's (Georgia) Legion, —
Phillips (Georgia) Legion, —
3d Georgia Battalion Sharpshooters, —

[1]A dash after the name of a unit indicates that the commanding officer's name is not known.

Humphreys' Brigade
BRIG. GEN. BENJAMIN G. HUMPHREYS
13th Mississippi, Maj. George L. Donald
17th Mississippi, —
18th Mississippi, Capt. William H. Lewis
21st Mississippi, Col. D. N. Moody

Bryan's Brigade
BRIG. GEN. GOODE BRYAN
10th Georgia, Col. Willis C. Holt
50th Georgia, Col. Peter McGlashan
51st Georgia, Col. Edward Ball
53d Georgia, Col. James P. Simms

FIELD'S DIVISION
MAJ. GEN. CHARLES W. FIELD

Jenkins' Brigade
BRIG. GEN. MICAH JENKINS
1st South Carolina, Col. James R. Hagood
2d South Carolina (Rifles), Col. Robert E. Bowen
5th South Carolina, Col. A. Coward
6th South Carolina, Col. John Bratton
Palmetto (South Carolina) Sharpshooters, Col. Joseph Walker

Law's Brigade
BRIG. GEN. EVANDER McIVOR LAW
4th Alabama, Col. Pinckney D. Bowles
15th Alabama, —
44th Alabama, Col. William F. Perry
47th Alabama, —
48th Alabama, Lieut. Col. William M. Hardwick

Anderson's Brigade
BRIG. GEN. GEORGE T. ANDERSON
7th Georgia, —
8th Georgia, —
9th Georgia, —
11th Georgia, —
59th Georgia, Lieut. Col. Bolivar H. Gee

Gregg's Brigade
BRIG. GEN. JOHN GREGG

3d Arkansas, Col. Van H. Manning
1st Texas, —
4th Texas, Col. John P. Bane
5th Texas, Lieut. Col. King Bryan

Benning's Brigade
BRIG. GEN. HENRY L. BENNING

2d Georgia, —
15th Georgia, Col. Dudley M. Du Bose
17th Georgia, —
20th Georgia, —

ARTILLERY
BRIG. GEN. E. PORTER ALEXANDER

Huger's Battalion
LIEUT. COL. FRANK HUGER

Fickling's (South Carolina) Battery
Moody's (Louisiana) Battery
Parker's (Virginia) Battery
J. D. Smith's (Virginia) Battery
Taylor's (Virginia) Battery
Woolfolk's (Virginia) Battery

Haskell's Battalion
MAJ. JOHN C. HASKELL

Flanner's (North Carolina) Battery
Garden's (South Carolina) Battery
Lamkin's (Virginia) Battery (unequipped)
Ramsay's (North Carolina) Battery

Cabell's Battalion
COL. HENRY C. CABELL

Callaway's (Georgia) Battery
Carlton's (Georgia) Battery
McCarthy's (Virginia) Battery
Manly's (North Carolina) Battery

SECOND ARMY CORPS
LIEUT. GEN. RICHARD S. EWELL

EARLY'S DIVISION
MAJ. GEN. JUBAL A. EARLY

Hays' Brigade
BRIG. GEN. HARRY T. HAYS
5th Louisiana, Lieut. Col. Bruce Menger
6th Louisania, Maj. William H. Manning
7th Louisiana, Maj. J. Moore Wilson
8th Louisiana, —
9th Lousiana, —

Pegram's Brigade
BRIG. GEN. JOHN PEGRAM
13th Virginia, Col. James B. Terrill
31st Virginia, Col. John S. Hoffman
49th Virginia, Col. J. Catlett Gibson
52d Virginia, —
58th Virginia, —

Gordon's Brigade
BRIG. GEN. JOHN B. GORDON
13th Georgia, —
26th Georgia, Col. Edmund N. Atkinson
31st Georgia, Col. Clement A. Evans
38th Georgia, —
60th Georgia, Lieut. Col. Thomas J. Berry
61st Georgia, —

JOHNSON'S DIVISION
MAJ. GEN. EDWARD JOHNSON

Stonewall Brigade
BRIG. GEN. JAMES A. WALKER
2d Virginia, Capt. Charles H. Stewart
4th Virginia, Col. William Terry
5th Virginia, —
27th Virginia, Lieut. Col. Charles L. Haynes
33d Virginia, —

Jones' Brigade
BRIG. GEN. JOHN M. JONES

21st Virginia, —
25th Virginia, Col. John C. Higginbotham
42d Virginia, —
44th Virginia, —
48th Virginia, —
50th Virginia, —

Steuart's Brigade
BRIG. GEN. GEORGE H. STEUART

1st North Carolina, Col. Hamilton A. Brown
3d North Carolina, Col. Stephen D. Thruston
10th Virginia, —
23d Virginia, —
37th Virginia, —

Stafford's Brigade
BRIG. GEN. LEROY A. STAFFORD

1st Louisiana, —
2d Louisiana, Col. Jesse M. Williams
10th Louisiana, —
14th Louisiana, —
15th Louisiana, —

RODES' DIVISION
MAJ. GEN. ROBERT E. RODES

Daniel's Brigade
BRIG. GEN. JUNIUS DANIEL

32d North Carolina, —
43d North Carolina, —
45th North Carolina, —
53d North Carolina, —
2d North Carolina Battalion, —

Doles' Brigade
BRIG. GEN. GEORGE DOLES
4th Georgia, —
12th Georgia, Col. Edward Willis
44th Georgia, Col. William H. Peebles

Ramseur's Brigade
BRIG. GEN. STEPHEN D. RAMSEUR
2d North Carolina, Col. William R. Cox
4th North Carolina, Col. Bryan Grimes
14th North Carolina, Col. R. Tyler Bennett
30th North Carolina, Col. Francis M. Parker

Battle's Brigade
BRIG. GEN. CULLEN A. BATTLE
3d Alabama, Col. Charles Forsyth
5th Alabama, —
6th Alabama, —
12th Alabama, —
26th Alabama, —

Johnston's Brigade
BRIG. GEN. ROBERT D. JOHNSTON
5th North Carolina, Col. Thomas M. Garrett
12th North Carolina, Col. Henry E. Coleman
20th North Carolina, Col. Thomas F. Toon
23d North Carolina, —

ARTILLERY
BRIG. GEN. ARMISTEAD L. LONG

Hardaway's Battalion[2]
LIEUT. COL. ROBERT A. HARDAWAY
Dance's (Virginia) Battery
Graham's (Virginia) Battery
C. B. Griffin's (Virginia) Battery
Jones' (Virginia) Battery
B. H. Smith's (Virginia) Battery

---

[2] Under the special direction of Col. J. Thomson Brown.

Braxton's Battalion

LIEUT. COL. CARTER M. BRAXTON

Carpenter's (Virginia) Battery
Cooper's (Virginia) Battery
Hardwicke's (Virginia) Battery

Nelson's Battalion

LIEUT. COL. WILLIAM NELSON

Kirkpatrick's (Virginia) Battery
Massie's (Virginia) Battery
Milledge's (Georgia) Battery

Cutshaw's Battalion[3]

MAJ. WILFRED E. CUTSHAW

Carrington's (Virginia) Battery
A. W. Garber's (Virginia) Battery
Tanner's (Virginia) Battery

Page's Battalion

MAJ. RICHARD C. M. PAGE

W. P. Carter's (Virginia) Battery
Fry's (Virginia) Battery
Page's (Virginia) Battery
Reese's (Alabama) Battery

---

[3] Under the special direction of Col. Thomas H. Carter.

THIRD ARMY CORPS
LIEUT. GEN. AMBROSE P. HILL

ANDERSON'S DIVISION
MAJ. GEN. RICHARD H. ANDERSON

Perrin's Brigade
BRIG. GEN. ABNER PERRIN

8th Alabama, —
9th Alabama, —
10th Alabama, —
11th Alabama, —
14th Alabama, —

Harris' Brigade
BRIG. GEN. NATHANIEL H. HARRIS

12th Mississippi, —
16th Mississippi, Col. Samuel E. Baker
l9th Mississippi, Col. Thomas J. Hardin
48th Mississippi, —

Mahone's Brigade
BRIG. GEN. WILLIAM MAHONE

6th Virginia, Lieut. Col. Henry W. Williamson
12th Virginia, Col. David A. Weisiger
16th Virginia, Lieut. Col. Richard O. Whitehead
41st Virginia, —
61st Virginia, Col. Virginius D. Groner

Wright's Brigade
BRIG. GEN. AMBROSE R. WRIGHT

3d Georgia, —
22d Georgia, —
48th Georgia, —
2d Georgia Battalion, Maj. Charles J. Moffett

Perry's Brigade
BRIG. GEN. EDWARD A. PERRY

2d Florida, —
5th Florida, —
8th Florida, —

HETH'S DIVISION
MAJ. GEN. HENRY HETH

Davis' Brigade
BRIG. GEN. JOSEPH R. DAVIS
2d Mississippi, —
11th Mississippi, —
42d Mississippi, —
55th North Carolina, —

Cooke's Brigade
BRIG. GEN. JOHN R. COOKE
15th North Carolina, —
27th North Carolina, —
46th North Carolina, —
48th North Carolina, —

Kirkland's Brigade
BRIG. GEN. WILLIAM W. KIRKLAND
11th North Carolina, —
26th North Carolina, —
44th North Carolina, —
47th North Carolina, —
52d North Carolina, —

Walker's Brigade
BRIG. GEN. HENRY H. WALKER
40th Virginia, —
47th Virginia, Col. Robert M. Mayo
55th Virginia, Col. William S. Christian
22d Virginia Battalion, —

Archer's Brigade
BRIG. GEN. JAMES J. ARCHER
13th Alabama, —
1st Tennessee (Provisional Army), Maj. Felix G. Buchanan
7th Tennessee, Lieut. Col. Samuel G. Shepard
14th Tennessee, Col. William McComb

WILCOX'S DIVISION
Maj. Gen. Cadmus M. Wilcox

Lane's Brigade
Brig. Gen. James H. Lane
7th North Carolina, Lieut. Col. William Lee Davidson
18th North Carolina, Col. John D. Barry
28th North Carolina, —
33d North Carolina, Lieut. Col. Robert V. Cowan
37th North Carolina, Col. William M. Barbour

Scales' Brigade
Brig. Gen. Alfred M. Scales
13th North Carolina, Col. Joseph H. Hyman
16th North Carolina, Col. William A. Stowe
22d North Carolina, —
34th North Carolina, Col. William L. J. Lowrance
38th North Carolina, Lieut. Col. John Ashford

McGowan's Brigade
Brig. Gen. Samuel McGowan
1st South Carolina (Provisional Army),
    Lieut. Col. Washington P. Shooter
12th South Carolina, Col. John L. Miller
13th South Carolina, Col. Benjamin T. Brockman
14th South Carolina, Col. Joseph N. Brown
1st South Carolina (Orr's Rifles), Lieut. Col. George McD. Miller

Thomas' Brigade
Brig. Gen. Edward L. Thomas
14th Georgia, —
35th Georgia, —
45th Georgia, —
49th Georgia, Lieut. Col. John T. Jordan

ARTILLERY
COL. R. LINDSAY WALKER

Poague's Battalion
LIEUT. COL. WILLIAM T. POAGUE
Richards' (Mississippi) Battery
Utterback's (Virginia) Battery
Williams' (North Carolina) Battery
Wyatt's (Virginia) Battery

Pegram's Battalion
LIEUT. COL. WILLIAM J. PEGRAM
Brander's (Virginia) Battery
Cayce's (Virginia) Battery
Ellett's (Virginia) Battery
Marye's (Virginia) Battery
Zimmerman's (South Carolina) Battery

McIntosh's Battalion
LIEUT. COL. DAVID G. McINTOSH
Clutter's (Virginia) Battery
Donald's (Virginia) Battery
Hurt's (Alabama) Battery
Price's (Virginia) Battery

Cutts' Battalion
COL. ALLEN S. CUTTS
Patterson's (Georgia) Battery
Ross' (Georgia) Battery
Wingfield's (Georgia) Battery

Richardson's Battalion
LIEUT. COL. CHARLES RICHARDSON
Grandy's (Virginia) Battery
Landry's (Louisiana) Battery
Moore's (Virginia) Battery
Penick's (Virginia) Battery

CAVALRY CORPS
MAJ. GEN. JAMES E. B. STUART

HAMPTON'S DIVISION
MAJ. GEN. WADE HAMPTON

Young's Brigade
BRIG. GEN. PIERCE M. B. YOUNG
7th Georgia, Col. William P. White
Cobb's (Georgia) Legion, Col. G. J. Wright
Phillips (Georgia) Legion, —
20th Georgia Battalion, Lieut. Col. John M. Millen
Jefferson Davis (Mississippi) Legion, —

Rosser's Brigade
BRIG. GEN. THOMAS L. ROSSER
7th Virginia, Col. Richard H. Dulany
11th Virginia, —
12th Virginia, Lieut. Col. Thomas B. Massie
35th Virginia Battalion, —

Butler's Brigade
BRIG. GEN. MATTHEW C. BUTLER
4th South Carolina, Col. B. Huger Rutledge
5th South Carolina, Col. John Dunovant
6th South Carolina, Col. Hugh K. Aiken

FITZHUGH LEE'S DIVISION
MAJ. GEN. FITZHUGH LEE

Lomax's Brigade
BRIG. GEN. LUNSFORD L. LOMAX
5th Virginia, Col. Henry C. Pate
6th Virginia, Col. John S. Green
15th Virginia, Col. Charles R. Collins

Wickham's Brigade

Brig. Gen. Williams C. Wickham

1st Virginia, —

2d Virginia, Col. Thomas T. Munford

3d Virginia, Col. Thomas H. Owen

4th Virginia, —

WILLIAM H. F. LEE'S DIVISION
Maj. Gen. William H. F. Lee

Chambliss' Brigade

Brig. Gen. John R. Chambliss, Jr.

9th Virginia, —

10th Virginia, —

13th Virginia, —

Gordon's Brigade

Brig. Gen. James B. Gordon

1st North Carolina, —

2d North Carolina, Col. Clinton M. Andrews

5th North Carolina, Col. Stephen B. Evans

HORSE ARTILLERY
Maj. R. Preston Chew

Breathed's Battalion

Maj. James Breathed

Hart's (South Carolina) Battery

Johnston's (Virginia) Battery

McGregor's (Virginia) Battery

Shoemaker's (Virginia) Battery

Thomson's (Virginia) Battery

FURTHER READING

Alexander, Edward Porter. *Fighting for the Confederacy: The Personal Recollections of General Edward Porter Alexander.* Edited by Gary W. Gallagher. Chapel Hill and London: University of North Carolina Press, 1989.

_____. *Military Memoirs of a Confederate.* Reprint. Bloomington: Indiana University Press, 1962.

Catton, Bruce. *A Stillness at Appomattox.* Garden City, N.Y.: Doubleday, 1955.

Cleaves, Freeman. *Meade of Gettysburg.* Norman: University of Oklahoma Press, 1960.

Dowdey, Clifford. *Lee's Last Campaign.* Boston: Little, Brown, 1960.

Early, Jubal A. *General Jubal A. Early: Autobiographical Sketch and Narrative of the War Between the States.* Reprint. Wilmington, N.C.: Broadfoot Press, 1989.

Eckenrode, H. J., and Bryan Conrad. *James Longstreet: Lee's War Horse.* Reprint. Chapel Hill and London: University of North Carolina Press, 1986.

Eckert, Ralph Lowell. *John Brown Gordon: Soldier, Southerner, American.* Baton Rouge: Louisiana State University Press, 1989.

Freeman, Douglas Southall. *Lee's Lieutenants: A Study in Command.* 3 vols. New York: Charles Scribner's Sons, 1942–44.

_____. *R. E. Lee: A Biography.* 4 vols. New York: Charles Scribner's Sons, 1934–35.

Gallagher, Gary W. *Stephen Dodson Ramseur: Lee's Gallant General.* Chapel Hill and London: University of North Carolina Press, 1985.

Gibbon, John. *Personal Recollections of the Civil War.* New York: G. P. Putnam's Sons, 1928.

Gordon, John B. *Reminiscences of the Civil War.* Reprint. Baton Rouge and London: Louisiana State University Press, 1993.

Grant, Ulysses S. *Papers of Ulysses S. Grant.* Edited by John Y. Simon. 20 vols to date. Carbondale and Edwardsville: Southern Illinois University Press, 1967– . Grant's correspondence during the Wilderness Campaign is in Vol. 10, January 1–May 31, 1864.

_____. *Personal Memoirs of Ulysses S. Grant.* 2 vols. New York: Charles L. Webster and Company, 1885.

Hassler, Warren W. *Commanders of the Army of the Potomac.* Baton Rouge: Louisiana State University Press, 1962.

Henderson, George Francis Robert. *The Campaign in the Wilderness of Virginia*. London: H. Rees, 1908.

Heth, Henry. *The Memoirs of Henry Heth*. Edited by James L. Morrison, Jr. Westport, CN: Greenwood Press, 1974.

Humphreys, Andrew Atkinson. *The Virginia Campaign of '64 and '65: The Army of the Potomac and the Army of the James*. New York: Charles Scribner's Sons, 1883.

Johnson, Robert Underwood, and Clarence Clough Buel, eds. *Battles and Leaders of the Civil War*. Reprint. 4 vols. New York: Thomas Yoseloff, Inc., 1956. Volume 4 contains accounts by participants in the Wilderness Campaign.

Jordan, David A. *Winfield Scott Hancock: A Soldier's Life*. Bloomington: Indiana University Press, 1988.

Lee, Robert E. *Lee's Dispatches: Unpublished Letters of General Robert E. Lee, C.S.A., to Jefferson Davis and the War Department of the Confederate States of America, 1862–65*. Edited by Douglas Southall Freeman and Grady McWhiney. New ed. Baton Rouge and London: Louisiana State University Press, 1995.

_____. *The Wartime Papers of Robert E. Lee*. Edited by Clifford Dowdey. Boston: Little, Brown, and Company, 1961.

Longstreet, James. *From Manassas to Appomattox: Memoirs of the Civil War in America*. Edited by James I. Robertson, Jr. New ed. Bloomington: Indiana University Press, 1960.

Lyman, Theodore. *With Grant and Meade from the Wilderness to Appomattox*. Edited by George Agassiz. Lincoln and London: University of Nebraska Press, 1994.

Marszalek, John F. *Sherman: A Soldier's Passion for Order*. New York: The Free Press, 1993.

Marvel, William. *Burnside*. Chapel Hill and London: University of North Carolina Press, 1991.

McAllister, Robert. *The Civil War Letters of General Robert McAllister*. Edited by James I. Robertson, Jr. New Brunswick, NJ: Rutgers University Press, 1965.

McFeely, William S. *Grant: A Biography*. New York: W. W. Norton and Company, 1981.

Meade, George G. *The Life and Letters of George Gordon Meade, Major General United States Army*. 2 vols. New York: Charles Scribner's Sons, 1913.

Piston, William Garrett. *Lee's Tarnished Lieutenant: James Longstreet and His Place in Southern History*. Athens and London: University of Georgia Press, 1987.

124 BATTLE IN THE WILDERNESS

Polley, Joseph Benjamin. *Hood's Texas Brigade, Its Marches, Its Battles, Its Achievements.* New York and Washington: The Neale Publishing Company, 1910.

Porter, Horace. *Campaigning with Grant.* Reprint. Bloomington: Indiana University Press, 1961.

Rhea, Gordon C. *The Battle of the Wilderness, May 5–6, 1864.* Baton Rouge and London: Louisiana State University Press, 1994.

Ripley, Edward Hastings. *Vermont General: The Unusual War Experiences of Edward Hastings Ripley, 1862–1865.* Edited by Otto Eisenschiml. New York: Devin-Adir, 1960.

Robertson, James I., Jr. *General A. P. Hill: The Story of a Confederate Warrior.* New York: Random House, 1987.

_____. *The Stonewall Brigade.* Baton Rouge: Louisiana State University Press, 1963.

Schaff, Morris. *The Battle of the Wilderness.* Boston: Houghton Mifflin and Company, 1910.

Scott, Robert Garth. *Into the Wilderness With the Army of the Potomac.* Bloomington: Indiana University Press, 1985.

Simpson, Harold B. *Gaines' Mill to Appomattox: Waco & McLennan County in Hood's Texas Brigade.* Waco, TX: Texian Press, 1988.

_____. *Hood's Texas Brigade: Lee's Grenadier Guard.* Waco, TX: Texian Press, 1970.

Sorrel, G. Moxley. *Recollections of a Confederate Staff Officer.* Reprint. Dayton, Ohio: Morningside Bookshop, 1978.

Steere. Edward. *The Wilderness Campaign.* Harrisburg, PA: Stackpole Company, 1960.

Swinton, William. *Campaigns of the Army of the Potomac: A Critical History of Operations in Virginia, Maryland and Pennsylvania, from the Commencement to the Close of the War, 1861–1865.* Revised Edition. New York: Charles Scribner's Sons, 1882.

Taylor, Emerson Gifford. *Gouverneur Kemble Warren: The Life and Letters of an American Soldier, 1830–1882.* Boston: Houghton Mifflin and Company, 1932.

Taylor, Walter H. *Four Years with General Lee.* Reprint. Bloomington: Indiana University Press, 1962.

Thomas, Emory M. *Bold Dragoon: The Life of J.E.B. Stuart.* New York: Random House, 1986.

Trudeau, Noah Andre. *Bloody Roads South: The Wilderness to Cold Harbor, May–June 1864.* Boston, Toronto, London: Little, Brown and Company, 1989.

Tucker, Glenn. *Hancock the Superb*. Indianapolis: Bobbs-Merrill
Company, 1960.

Waugh, John C. *The Class of 1846 From West Point to Appomattox:
Stonewall Jackson, George McClellan and their Brothers*. New
York: Warner Books, 1994.

Wert, Jeffry D. *General James Longstreet: The Confederacy's Most
Controversial Soldier—A Biography*. New York: Simon & Schuster,
1993.

Wilkinson, Warren. *Mother, May You Never See the Sights I Have Seen:
The Fifty-Seventh Massachusetts Veteran Volunteers in the Army of
the Potomac, 1864–1865*. New York: Harper & Row, 1990.

INDEX